Lingerie Secrets

Sew a perfect fit fo[r every body]

Jan Bones

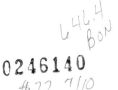

Published by

krause
publications
700 East State Street • Iola, WI 54990-0001
715/445-2214 • FAX: 715/445-4087 www.krause.com

Edited by Jo Phillip
Book design by Donna Mummery
Cover design by Joe Perz
Photos and illustrations by Jan Bones

Please call or write for our free catalog of publications. Our toll-free number to place an order or obtain a free catalog is 800-258-0929 or please use our regular business telephone 715-445-2214 for editorial comment and further information.

Contact Jan Bones by email: jbones3@home.com;
or by mail at Box 23003, Winnipeg, Manitoba R3T5S3, Canada.

Printed in the United States of America
Library of Congress Catalog Number: 99-69481
ISBN 0-87341-852-2

Acknowledgments

Thank you...

...to the people at Krause Publications, for the work they do so well.

...to my family and friends, for being interested in what I do, and for encouraging me in every adventure.

...to Donna Pascal and Janet Menec for their valuable time and expertise. Reading, editing and correcting the original manuscript was a task they willingly accepted. I think they did an amazing job, considering that they worked with a photoless manuscript! Their ideas and excellent suggestions have been incorporated into the book.

...to Carolyn McLaughlin and Marilyn Halliday for proofing and testing the drafting directions. They suggested better ways to communicate directions, and they caught errors I missed. A valuable contribution to this book.

...to Melody Windsor, Linda Parenty and Kim White for their bodies! We laughed, we took pictures, and now these wonderful ladies grace the pages of the book.

...to George for being excited for me when the opportunity to write this book came about...for taking photographs...for teaching me about cameras and lenses...for finding the Cadillac of slide sorters at an auction sale...for proofreading...for being there every step of the way.

From the Author   July 2000

My Mom taught me to sew when I was young. I learned secrets from her that seemed to be magic. She taught me how to make felt puppets, how to sew doll clothes, how to embroider on tea towels—and Mom helped me make my first hipster miniskirt.

Mrs. Johanna Wilson taught Home Economics sewing classes in the '60s. From her, I learned about perfection. Anne and Ernie Braun gave me my first opportunity to teach sewing classes, and this expanded my fascination with the entire arena of pattern design and sewing. Their fabric store was where I gained the knowledge of sewing that I still value today. As I continued my education at the University of Manitoba in the '70s, Professor Shannon taught us all to work very hard. "No fuss no muss," she could be heard to say, "just do it well."

One of the most satisfying activities in my teaching life has been to watch students learn. Absorbing new ideas, trying them out, making changes along the way and achieving success—this is a rewarding process to watch. A student once told me that in class she "learned to have the confidence to try." What a perfect result!

The information in this book has been accumulated over a lifetime of teaching students to create their own patterns and to sew. I hope you, too, are inspired.

I hope that you, too, gain the confidence to try. I also wish you the joy of sewing, and the patience and persistence to work things out when they are not perfect.

To all my family, friends and students from the past, present and future, you have made a tremendously positive difference in my life. I thank you.

Jan Bones

Table of Contents

Introduction

Patterns, fabrics and notions are the basic ingredients for wonderful lingerie designs, and they can be assembled to create infinite combinations. This book is all about creating lingerie that you will treasure for yourself, and that others will be thrilled to receive as a gift. I am confident that, by following the photos and step by step directions for each design, you will successfully learn to sew lovely lingerie.

I'm delighted to have the chance to share with you the many fitting and sewing tricks included in each chapter. Sometimes the smallest detail makes a project that much more successful and fun to sew—and I am glad to have been able to learn some of these tricks along the way, to save you the extra step! You will learn how to select fabric, how to choose stitches, how to sew lace, and much more.

This book offers you three approaches for making your own special lingerie.

First, patterns are included for a knit camisole and nightie, a bra top, classic panties, and maternity panties. They are simple shapes, which have been developed and tested with the help of many women to achieve the best fit possible. These patterns are in half-scale, ready for you to simply photocopy to full scale. They are then ready at your fingertips for layout on fabric. The ideal fit is different for every figure—and for every personality. We all have our own personal preferences about garment ease, length and silhouette. To help you in this area, there are many fitting ideas and suggestions throughout each chapter.

Next, you will learn to redesign and recycle your commercial pattern favorites into wonderful new lingerie classics. The boxer, the slip and the maternity nightie all invite you to sample this approach.

Third, the technique of drafting patterns is introduced in this book. Pattern drafting incorporates the measurements of an individual figure into a series of drafting steps to create an individual pattern for the figure's unique size. I believe pattern drafting is a valuable technique to master in working toward successful fit. Our bodies do not fit a standard range of sizes; we all have variations and differences. Some of the variations we like and others we like a little less; nonetheless, we need to work with what we have!

Successful patterns, fitting and sewing are all within your reach.

Sewing is a world without limits. The simplest pair of boxers may start a young person on the road to a lifetime of sewing. A June wedding may inspire the more experienced sewer to create luxurious nighties for the new bride. The simple designs in this book may present the perfect opportunity for a Mom or a Grandma to pass sewing along to another generation. We have unlimited opportunities to let our creative sides shine through, and to see rewarding results.

No matter what your sewing aspirations, add the designing and sewing of lingerie to your list of accomplishments. You will love it!

Chapter 1

Fabrics and Notions

Fabrics for lingerie may be divided into two groups: woven fabrics and knit fabrics.

Woven fabrics are made when crosswise and lengthwise yarns are interlaced. Many people recognize classic fabrics such as broadcloth, muslin and gingham. Far beyond these classics however, are voile, satin, brocade, seersucker, crepe, pique, chiffon and the microfiber fabrics. Any or all of these could be great fabric selections for lingerie, on account of their weight, fiber content and hand. Hand is defined as the way the fabric feels when it is touched and handled.

Cotton, polyester, rayon, silk and countless combinations of these fibers are all good choices for lingerie designs. Cotton batiste is a thin, cool and smooth fabric; rayon challis is a medium weight fabric with a pleasing texture and feel; polyester satin-backed crepe is heavier, has a fluid drape and a slippery feel; silk charmeuse is slippery, rich feeling and pure elegance. These are only a few examples in the range of woven fabric choices.

Woven fabric for lingerie: 100% cotton voile, 100% cotton calico and 50/50 cotton polyester broadcloth.

These fabrics are all 100% polyester.

100% silk fabric—a treat against the skin!

Some of these fabrics would traditionally be used for blouses and dresses. When you visit a fabric store, examine fabrics with a new perspective and a little extra thought. Perhaps a cotton batiste camisole would be fun, or a satin-backed crepe nightie. What fabric might best suit the boxer or bra top? The natural fibers—cotton, linen and silk—feel cooler against the skin because they allow air to pass through them. The man-made fibers, polyester and nylon, hold in body heat and do not allow the passage of air. They don't breathe as well. These fabrics can make the body feel hot. The primary thought to keep in mind when choosing a fabric for lingerie is the feel. Ask yourself, "do I like the fiber content? Does the fabric have a pleasing texture and hand? Would I like this fabric next to my skin? How would I feel wearing this?"

The wonderful secret of woven fabric for the nighties and camisoles drafted in Chapter 4 is the use of the bias direction for cutting. This technique for cutting fabric allows the garment to have some degree of give vertically and horizontally, on an otherwise stable fabric. A garment that has been cut on the bias drapes and shapes over the figure's curves. A bias cut even allows for some flexibility of fit, because the fabric smoothes itself over different figures' curves.

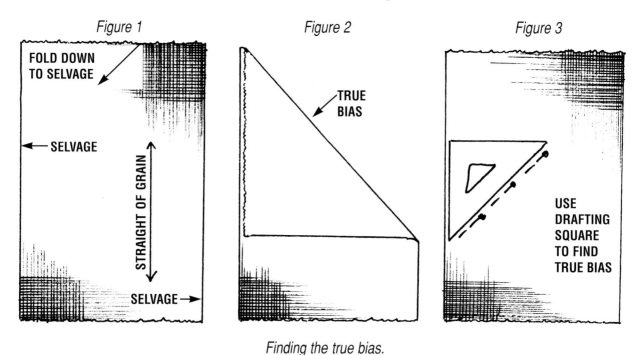

Finding the true bias.

One way to find the "true bias" is to fold the fabric so the crosswise cut edges line up to the selvage. The fold created is the "true bias" (Figures 1 and 2).

An alternate way to find the "true bias" is to line up the square corner of an equilateral drafting triangle to the selvage. The angled edge of the triangle is 45 degrees from the selvage. Mark this line with pins or chalk if you like (Figure 3).

Terry toweling, chenille and quilted cottons are some typical choices for housecoats and robes. The patterns for these designs generally indicate they be cut on the straight of grain to create the most attractive hang of the garment. Boxer shorts are a lingerie design best cut on the traditional straight of grain in the woven fabrics.

Woven fabrics vary in width. Flannelette and some madras-type plaids are 36" (92cm) wide. Most fabrics are 45" (115cm) and 60" (150cm). There are cottons, sheetings and percales that come in 100" (254cm) and 120" (305cm).

Knit fabrics are made when yarns are interlooped to produce a fabric with some degree of stretch. Some knits are tubular, and for easier pattern layout, the tube may need to be cut open. Many other knits are available in flat form. The widths of these various fabrics range from approximately 24" to 60" (61cm to 150cm).

Their comfort, stretch and easy care make knits a natural choice for lingerie. Knits allow for either a body-hugging fit or a graceful, flowing silhouette. They usually have a soft hand and an attractive appearance. Quite durable, they are available in different fiber contents. Five types of knits are described here for use in lingerie designs:

1. **Single knit fabrics**, also called flat knits, are an excellent choice for panties, nighties and camisoles. They have their greatest stretch horizontally, and they offer minimal vertical stretch. The right side of a single knit fabric has definite vertical lines called wales, while the wrong side has horizontal lines called courses. Hand knitters would recognize this fabric as the "stockinette stitch." Cotton and blends of cotton/polyester and cotton/lycra are popular fiber choices. They have a cool feel and are lightweight. If there is a knitted-in pattern or a print, the fabric's right side is easy to distinguish. When in doubt, the right and wrong sides may be found by stretching the fabric. When stretched across, the fabric edge rolls to the right side.

Single knits, some 100% cotton, some polyester/cotton blends.

Various novelty knits.

These examples are all 100% cotton interlock.

2. Interlock knit has a smooth feel, with no difference between the right and wrong side—unless it has a printed pattern. The edges of the fabric stay flat and do not curl when stretched, making it an easy fabric to cut and sew. Interlock has its greatest stretch horizontally across the fabric, and is often heavier than a single knit. Cotton interlock is one of the best choices for the lining crotch of panties. It is cool and soft. Camisoles and nighties are cozy in cotton or cotton/polyester interlock. Interlock of 100% polyester has a smooth hand, travels well, and is very easy to care for. It has a wonderful drape for long nighties and gowns.

3. Rib knits have definite lengthwise lines on both sides of the fabric. Rib knitting creates a more elastic fabric. There is a great variety in the weights and fiber contents available. Commonly used for the neckband and cuffs on t-shirts, rib knits are warm and durable.

Rib knits.

Antron® nylon tricot.

Such lingerie items as boxers, nighties and camisoles would be suitable for rib knit fabrics.

4. Tricot is a warp knit fabric with many unique characteristics. Softness, crease resistance, stretch and a pleasing drape combine to make it an especially appealing fabric. Nylon is the man-made fiber most often used for tricot, because the result is strong, and it wears extremely well. Tricot fabrics have slippery surfaces that make them good choices for slips, panties, camisoles and nighties.

Colors range from white and pastel to black. Tricot may also be available in prints, and in the intense teal or red colors. Both the weight of the yarn and the tightness of stitches determine the fabric thickness, and tricots vary from sheer (15 denier) to opaque (40 denier). Antron® is an anti-static finish for tricot with a beautiful luster.

Nylon tricot should be pressed at a low heat setting on the iron. It is heat sensitive, and could melt at high temperatures. The right side of tricot may be found in the same way as has been described for single knits. One disadvantage of nylon tricot is that it absorbs little moisture and it doesn't breathe—so it may make the wearer feel very warm on a hot day. Nylon is also a color scavenger in the wash—be careful to separate colors.

5. **Two-way stretch knits** are unique because they stretch both horizontally across the width of the fabric, as well as vertically. Patterns that call for two-way stretch fabrics differ from patterns for single knits in that the two-way knit patterns are designed to accommodate the multi-directional stretch of the fabric. Two-way stretch fabrics vary in weight and fiber content, and are popular for panties, bodysuits and sports bras. Cotton/spandex and nylon/spandex are common blends. Stretch lace fabrics are often two-way stretch.

Two-way stretch knits.

Nylon/spandex two-way stretch lace fabric.

100% nylon lingerie lace.

100% polyester bridal lace.

Narrow lace trims.

100% nylon lingerie lace.

Notions

Notions for lingerie include thread, lace, elastic and ribbon. Each plays an important role in the construction of any design.

1. High quality **thread** is indispensable for all sewing. With lingerie, it is essential, because the garments are washed and worn often. Polyester thread is suitable for sewing most fabrics. Cotton thread is an excellent choice when sewing 100% cotton fabric, either knit or woven. Cotton thread is also a suitable choice for silk fabrics.

It is always a good idea to sew a test seam with the proposed thread on your fabric. This quick step allows you to check machine tension and needle size, as well as to try the proposed length and type of stitch. Of course, you will also see whether the thread color is a good match.

2. **Lace** is used to add elegance, luxury and sometimes function to lingerie. Polyester, cotton and nylon laces are preferable for their long life and washability. When selecting lace, pay extra attention to the feel. Look for the smooth, soft laces, as they are the most comfortable next to the skin. Avoid crispy or stiff laces—they are uncomfortable to wear, and these characteristics often do not wash out, but rather, remain over the life of the garment. In addition to their being uncomfortable, crisp laces tend to cause slips to "walk up" the legs when worn over pantyhose.

Lace trims are made in widths anywhere from 1/4" (.6cm) to 6" (15.7cm). Some have straight edges, some scalloped or pointed edges. Some have simple motifs, while others are two-colored, elegant designs. Lace also comes as yardage in varying widths, patterns, weights and of course prices.

3. Elastics are used at the leg and waist of panties, at the waist of slips and boxers and at the back of nighties. Elastics offer a fairly simplified solution for a personalized fit, and more comfortable lingerie.

The width of elastics vary from 1/8" (.3cm) to as much as 5" (13cm). They often have texture, color and pattern variation. The weight of elastic varies from light lingerie types, to heavier pajama elastics that may used for boxers.

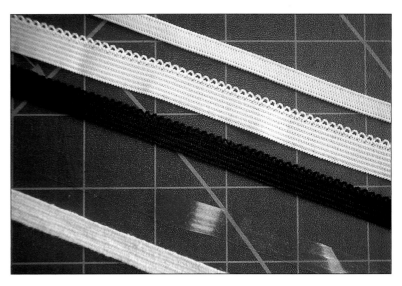

Elastics: knitted, picot edge (x2), clear and braided.

A "picot edge" is a term referring to the narrow decorative looped edge on lingerie elastic. "Plush back" elastic has been made with one soft and fuzzy side, a great option for the band on the bra top. As with lace, elastics made with polyester, cotton or nylon are best. One of these fibers is generally combined with rubber or spandex to produce the elastic.

I recommend knitted elastics, because when they are stretched, they maintain their original width. This quality allows easier, neater, more accurate sewing, which results in a professional looking finished garment.

Braided elastics are also available—however, they become narrower when stretched. This makes accurate stitching more difficult, because the edge of the elastic moves away from its original location. To check your elastic, or to determine what you are looking at in a store, simply stretch the elastic a comfortable amount and examine the effect on the piece's width. Cotton swimsuit elastic is braided. It is soft and unbleached, so it is beige in color.

Elastics: pajama (x2) and knitted (x2).

Clear elastic (also known as plastic or diaper elastic) is another choice for lingerie. Made of 100% polyurethane, it is 1/3 the thickness of regular elastic, and it is washable and durable. A width of 3/8" is common to use on the edges of nighties and panties. For comfort's sake, clear elastic is best covered with fabric. It tends to feel sticky next to the skin.

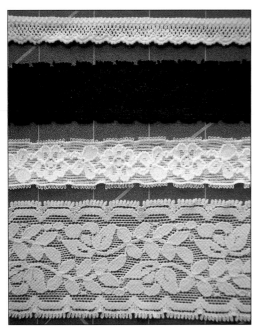

Elastic stretch laces are also available for lingerie. They feel soft and stretch easily— so, they may not feel as snug to the body as other elastics. Widths of approximately 3/8" to 2" (1cm to 5cm) are available in a variety of colors and elastic stretch laces are often used at the waist of panties and slips and necklines of nighties. They usually have floral, all-over patterns that add a decorative touch to a design. Soft elastic stretch laces are also available in yardage, perfect for bodices and the front of maternity panties.

Elastic stretch lace trim.

Ideas for straps: satin ribbon, adjustable straps, velvet cord, jacquard ribbon and picot edge ribbon, jacquard ribbon.

4. **Ribbon** is most often used for straps on camisoles and nighties. Polyester is the most common fiber content, and widths generally start at 1/8" (.3cm). A complete range of colors is available. Ribbons may be satin on one or both sides, they may be very dainty and sheer, they may have a jacquard pattern woven into them, or they may have a picot edge with tiny thread loops. Ribbon is also available in ready-made adjustable straps. They are packaged in pairs and have plastic sliders, which permit adjustment. Their widths range from 3/8" to 1/2" (1cm to 1.3cm). They are generally available in beige, black and white.

Preshrinking

All washable woven and knit fabrics, lace and notions, should be washed before the garment is sewn, to prevent the effects of shrinkage. The crosswise ends of woven fabrics fray. For this reason, take the worthwhile step of serging or zigzagging these ends before washing.

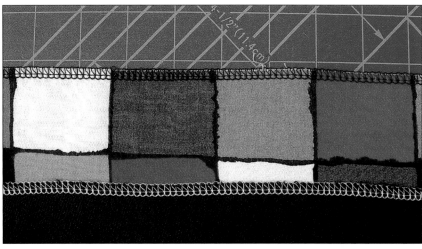

Serge the raw edges of woven fabric before pre-shrinking.

Nylon tricot and single knit fabrics curl to the right side when stretched. Machine stitching the raw edges together controls this rolling, so that cutting and sewing is much simpler. While these are extra steps to take, they save time in the long run, because they keep the fabric flat, making it easier to handle.

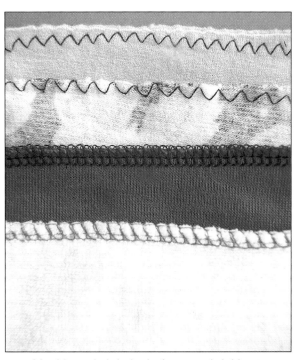

Machine stitch knits before preshrinking to prevent rolling.

Preshrinking may be done in one of three ways:

1. Place the lace or elastic in a small bowl filled with hot water, or place fabric into a sink. Leave it to soak a few minutes. Then, gently squeeze out the water and lay the item flat on a towel to air dry. Tumbling the fabric in a dryer for a few minutes removes wrinkles and produces a beautiful, smooth fabric, ready for layout and cutting.

2. Laces may also be preshrunk by pressing carefully with the correct heat setting on your iron. Use steam for even better results.

If your iron has an extra boost of steam, hold the iron slightly above the lace and steam it to preshrink. This is a quick method—but take care to test a sample first, as nylon laces melt if the iron is too hot.

3. Wash and dry your fabric in the machines. Place notions into a zippered laundry bag before washing them in the machine. If the finished garment will be dried in the dryer, then dry the lace that way as well. However, it is worth noting that laces, elastics, ribbons and notions of all kinds last longer if the garments on which they are sewn are hung to dry.

Pull yarn across fabric and cut to straighten.

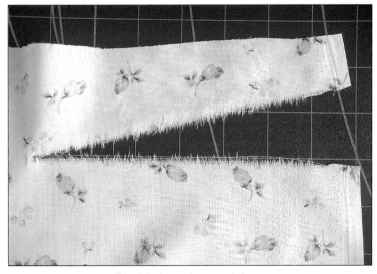

Cut along dominant line to straighten.

Straighten both ends of the cut fabric:

Wovens: All woven fabric available for lingerie should be straightened before sewing. This enhances the drape and hang of the designs. One yarn should run across the entire width of the fabric at each end. This is done in one of three ways:

1. Cut through the selvage and pull one of the crosswise yarns in the fabric. You may need to pull a little at a time and cut along the yarn as you go, or you may be able to pull the entire yarn. What you must do is create a pucker all the way across the fabric, which gives you a guide for cutting.

2. Cut along a dominant line in a fabric with a woven-in plaid, like gingham.

3. Cut through the selvage (tightly woven edge of the fabric) and rip the fabric across its entire width. Then, cut the selvage on the other edge. The ripping line will naturally fall along one yarn. This method is usually best on light to medium weight, plain weave fabrics. This ripping action can distort fabrics and create puckers. If possible, test the ripping to see whether the result will be satisfactory. Method 1 or 2 may be preferred.

Rip fabric end to straighten.

Check the alignment of the yarns of the fabric:

Now that each end of the fabric follows along one yarn, the fabric grain may be straightened. Straight grain means that the lengthwise yarns and the crosswise yarns are perpendicular, or square, with one another. Fold the fabric in half, align the two selvages and examine the cut ends. For perfectly straight grain, the edges must lie on top of one another and create a square corner with selvage and fold.

Following are two of the problems you might encounter, and their solutions to produce a fabric with straight grain.

Problem No. 1: The raw edges at each end of the fabric do not match.

Solution: Lay fabric as a single layer, and pull in the direction of the arrows, along the bias direction of the fabric, until the fabric is straight.

The raw edges do not match.

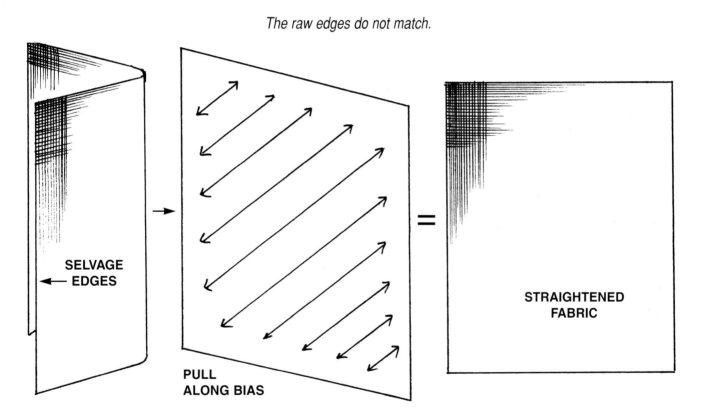

SELVAGE
← EDGES

PULL
ALONG BIAS

STRAIGHTENED
FABRIC

Problem No. 2: The cut ends match, but they are not square to the fold or selvage of the fabric.

Solution: Leave the fabric folded, and pull in the direction of the arrows until the layers of fabric are straight.

The cut edges match, but they are not square.

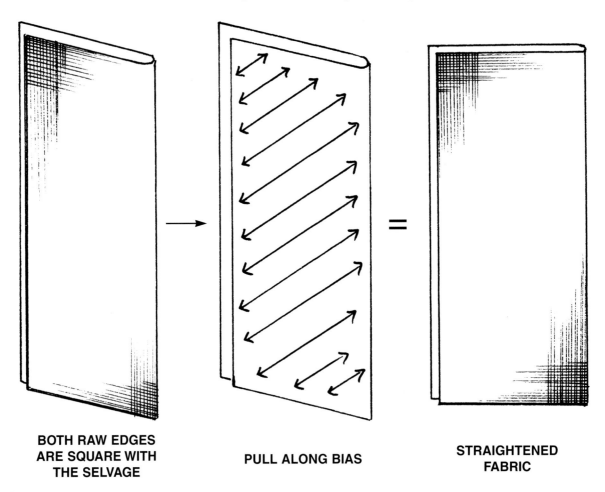

BOTH RAW EDGES ARE SQUARE WITH THE SELVAGE   **PULL ALONG BIAS**   **STRAIGHTENED FABRIC**

Knits: After a knit fabric has been preshrunk, it may appear twisted. The solution is to remove the row of machine basting I recommended you sew to hold the two raw edges together during the preshrinking step. Remove it by pulling out the threads, or by cutting off the slight amount of fabric and the sewing threads at the same time.

Good quality knits are made up of straight lengthwise rows of stitches. Once knit fabrics are washed, they may shrink slightly and upon examination, some knits may now appear to have crooked lengthwise rows of stitches. Pressing, gentle pulling and stretching help to straighten the fabric. However, the fabric will only relax again in future washings. The garment will become slightly crooked again, so it seems best to use the fabric as it is after preshrinking, and not make attempts at straightening.

Chapter 2

Sewing Equipment

G ood, high quality tools and equipment are imperative to the creation of a quality garment.

Needles

Needles for both sewing machines and sergers are available in different types and sizes. Needles should be changed frequently to ensure that the fabric being sewn remains in top quality condition. If you accidentally sew through something thick, or you hit a pin and hear the "clunk" of the needle hitting metal, stop. Change the needle immediately. Damaged needles cause holes when the fabric is being sewn.

Here are some of my recommended needle choices for various sewing tasks:

❖ Size 10 (70) ball point is recommended for lightweight knits, size 12 for medium weights.
❖ Size 10 (70) sharps or universal needles are used for woven fabrics like cotton batiste or polyester crepe, size 12 for medium weights.
❖ The Micro-tex needle is recommended for microfiber fabrics. It is also an effective problem solver on fabrics that create skipped stitches.
❖ A "stretch" needle may be helpful for fabrics that contain spandex. This needle has been designed to penetrate through the fabric to allow proper stitch formation.
❖ Twin needles are an interesting alternative for hems and decorative applications. These needles are threaded with two top threads and the usual one bobbin thread. The resulting stitch has two beautifully even straight stitches on the right side, and a small zigzag showing on the back side of the fabric.

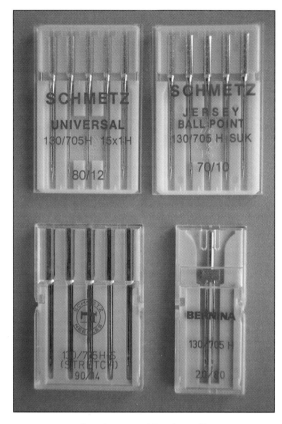

Sewing machine needles.

Twin needle stitching.

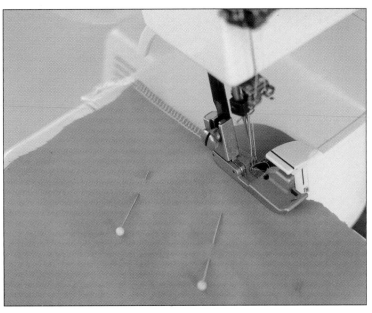

Pins

Pins with glass or plastic heads are easiest to hold and easiest to find. They come in a variety of useful lengths. Lingerie fabrics are generally lightweight, and the pins used during sewing must suit the fabric's weight. Test your pins on the selected fabric to be sure they pass through the fabric smoothly. Pins may have—or, with use, they may develop—burrs or snags at the tips. Throw these pins out, or they will damage your fabric.

When sewing with a machine, remove the pins from

Pins are used 2-1/2 inches from the cut edges.

the fabric before they travel under the presser foot. This prevents broken needles, broken pins, and holes in the fabric, and ensures safe sewing.

When using a serger, pins must never be in the path of the stitch line—but some fabrics require the accuracy pins allow. A helpful tip is to place pins 2-1/2" (6.5cm) from the cut edges. This holds the fabric together, but keeps the pins well out of the way of the serger needles and cutting blade. Alternately, a row of hand basting close to the stitching line ensures stitching accuracy.

Scissors.

Cutting Tools

All cutting tools must cut cleanly and accurately. Lingerie seams need little or no trimming, and so the original cutting lines are often the final edges in the garment. Traditional bent-handled shears, open-handled scissors, like Fiskars Soft Touch Scissors, and cutting wheels and mats are all excellent choices. When cutting slippery, lightweight fabrics with a wheel and mat, I like to cut along a ruler or a curve to give the most accurate edge.

Cut with a cutting wheel along a curved edge ruler.

Cut with a cutting wheel along a straight edged ruler.

Cutting mats do become rough with long time use. Drag a scrap of any delicate fabric over the mat to determine whether it is appropriate for use on the lingerie fabric you have selected to cut. The entire piece of fabric must rest on top of the cutting surface. If it hangs over the edge, shifting and distortion will cause inaccuracies in the shape of the final pieces.

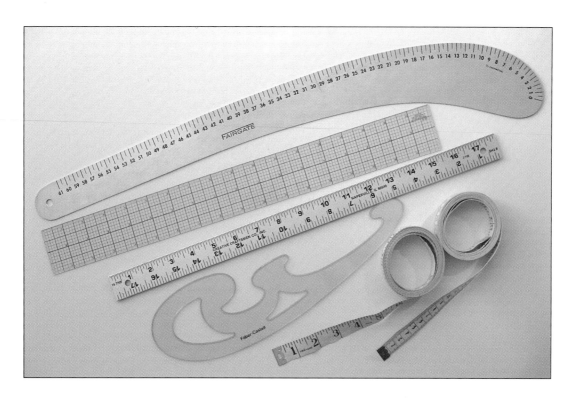

Drafting tools. From top to bottom: metal hip curve ruler, clear plastic ruler, metal ruler, French curve and dressmaker's tape measures.

Helpful drafting tools

1. **Dressmaker's tape measure.** These are usually made of fabric or plastic and are flexible to measure the body.

2. **18" to 24" (45cm-60cm) ruler.** Metal or clear plastic rulers with easy-to-read markings are easiest to use for measuring and drawing straight lines.

3. **Drafting square.** Usually clear plastic, this tool allows you to draw perfectly square corners. A large square is best.

4. **French curve,** 8" to 12" (20cm-30cm) in length. This tool comes in many sizes and shapes, and may be plastic, metal or wood. You want gentle and smooth curves in a pattern, and the French curve helps to make those more professionally shaped kinds of patterns.

5. **Metal hip curve ruler** (optional but great). For long side seam shapes, large sweeping hems and graceful neckline shapes, this curve is perfect. It is metal, and has measurement markings along one edge.

6. **Pencils** (lead for drafting and red for corrections).

7. **Paper** (ideas: brown paper, plain newsprint, tissue, tracing paper marked with 1" grid markings).

8. **Eraser, clear tape**, **paper** and **scissors**.

Chapter 3

Sewing Machines, Sergers and Techniques

Lingerie designs, in all woven and knit fabrics, can be sewn by using the straight and zigzag stitch combinations on a regular sewing machine. All sewing machine makes and models, from the simplest to the most elaborate, will sew all your favorite designs beautifully. The various seams produced by a serger are also excellent for lingerie. If you have both types of machines, you will be able to use the features of both to sew panties, nighties, slips, boxers and much more.

A clean, oiled and well-maintained sewing machine ensures trouble-free sewing. Open arm sewing machines often have a small table extension to provide you a larger sewing surface. This extra surface may be helpful for lingerie fabrics, which are often lightweight and slippery. The regular presser feet for sewing machines and sergers are most often used. I also make mention of other feet for specific techniques in the various chapters throughout this book.

The Sewing Machine

Straight stitches and various zigzag stitches are employed in the sewing of beautiful lingerie. The following tips will help you to make the most effective use of these stitches.

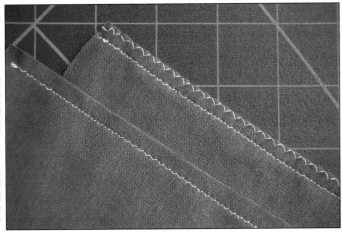

A seam with two rows of stitching.   *Various zigzag stitches on seams.*

Types of Stitches and Seams on the Sewing Machine

On both knit and woven fabrics: **A seam with two rows of stitching** is durable and easy to make. Here are the steps:

1. Place fabrics right sides together.
2. Sew a row of the narrowest zigzag at the 3/8" (1cm) seam allowance. On a sewing machine with a zigzag range of 0-4, a good setting for this zigzag stitch would be 1/2 to 1. Be sure to reinforce at the beginning and end of the stitching line, to create a more

durable seam. Stretch the fabric slightly when completing the row of the narrowest zigzag to give extra flexibility to the seam.

3. Finish the raw edges by sewing a medium width plain zigzag or a multiple zigzag, without stretching the fabric as you sew. Take care to feed the fabric evenly through the sewing machine so that the zigzag stitches lie evenly over the raw edges. A good width for this line of zigzag is a setting of 2-1/2 to 3-1/2. Vary the width according to your fabric and your preference. The widest width of zigzag is too wide because it creates a side-to-side pucker in lightweight fabrics, making a bulky, unattractive seam.

Tip: For fabrics that roll, I often finish the raw edges first by sewing the medium width zigzag over them. Because this controls the rolling and keeps the fabric lying flat, the regular seam line is much easier to sew.

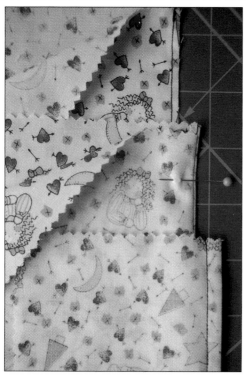

Steps for the French seam.

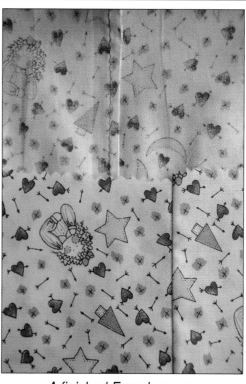

A finished French seam.

The French seam is made up of two rows of straight stitching. It is most often used on lightweight, woven fabric. The French seam works beautifully on both straight grain and bias cut seams. This type of seam completely encloses all raw edges, and results in a perfect, couture finish.

To create a French seam, follow these steps:

1. Place two garment pieces wrong sides together, and sew a 1/4" (0.6cm) seam. Press the seams to one side.

2. Place these same pieces right sides together, and sew a 3/8" (1cm) seam. Press the seam allowances toward the back of the garment, and the seam is complete. Note: these seam amounts are intended for use when the original seam allowance is 5/8" (1.5cm).

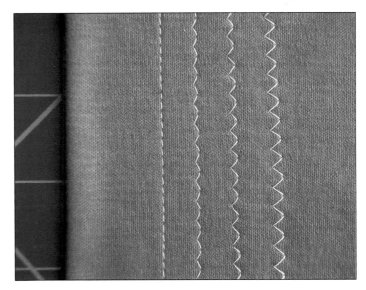

Various widths of the zigzag stitch.

The plain zigzag stitch is used to sew elastic. Different widths of zigzag are used for different types of elastic. The elastics commonly used in this book range in width from 1/4" to 1" (.6cm to 2.5cm).

For the narrow elastics of 1/4" to 3/8" (.6cm to 1cm), I use a zigzag width setting of 1-1/2 to 2, when the widest setting is 4.

For the 3/4" to 1" (2cm to 2.5cm) wide elastic, the zigzag width may be 2-1/2 to 3.

The key to successfully sewing elastic is to use an appropriate stitch length. The zigzag must allow the elastic to bounce back, or "recover," to its original shape after being sewn. As an example, my sewing machine's stitch length ranges from 0 to 4. At the 3 setting, it produces an excellent zigzag length. When zigzag stitches are too close together, they oversew the elastic. The elastic "grows" because it stays in the stretched out position when oversewn. Try a sample and make note of the stitch length that produces good results on your machine.

Another important detail for successfully sewing elastic is correct placement of stitching; line up the zigzag along the elastic's edge, so one point of the zigzag sews over the edge and the other point sews into the elastic without piercing a strand of spandex or rubber. This way, the sewing machine needle travels through the elastic fewer times. In addition, there is a consistent straight edge to follow and the final appearance is neat. Use thread to match the elastic color for an invisible effect.

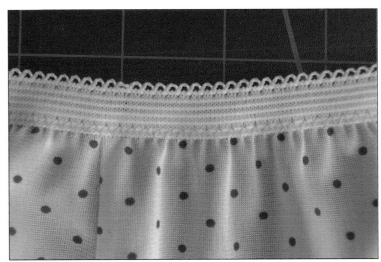

Placement of the zigzag on the edge of the elastic.

Regular presser foot and embroidery foot.

I often use the embroidery presser foot, or the satin stitch foot, on my sewing machine to sew 1/4" to 3/8" (.6cm to 1cm) wide elastic. This foot has a space, or channel, on the bottom that has been designed to glide over a satin stitch—and it glides over elastic in the same way. The idea is the same as the buttonhole foot; it is made with two grooves on the bottom, cleverly designed to glide smoothly over the two zigzag stitching lines that produce the buttonhole.

The multiple zigzag is an excellent choice for applying lace onto fabric. This stitch is sometimes called the "three step zigzag" or the "serpentine stitch." About three straight stitches up and three stitches down are made when forming the zigzag, allowing the lace to lie flat and the stitches to be almost invisible. Set the stitch width anywhere from medium to wide.

Multiple zigzag the lace to the knit fabric's hem edge.

This stitch can be used to sew along the straight edge of a lace trim or along the wavy edge of scalloped lace. You could also sew around the circumference of an appliqué piece of lace. Always pin within the lace, or far enough away from the lace edge so that you can completely avoid the pins while stitching. If you must pin in the area where you will eventually sew, remove the pins as you go.

The stretch stitch makes a strong, stretchy seam. It is formed when the sewing machine moves forward a few stitches and then backwards a few stitches. It may combine straight and zigzag stitches. The resulting seam is strong and stretchy, yet thick and somewhat rigid. I only recommend this stitch for very heavyweight fabrics.

Starting the Seam

Fabrics used to create lingerie are often lightweight, and starting a seam neatly and accurately is important. One approach involves placing the fabric under the presser foot and turning the sewing machine hand wheel twice to anchor the thread into the fabric. Then, use one hand to guide the fabric in front of presser foot and the other hand to hold the threads behind the presser foot. Pull the threads behind the presser foot to start the seam smoothly.

Another good way to start a seam begins with a 3" square of muslin. Fold the square in half. Place the strip lengthwise under the presser foot at mid-strip, aligning its long, raw edges with the correct seam guideline on the throat plate. Start sewing and as you come to the bottom end of the strip, stop and line up the beginning of the garment seam with the strip. Sew onto the fabric, back tack once or twice and then continue and complete the seam. This method gives you something to hold as you begin the seam, and enables you to sew it evenly. Later, just clip away the muslin.

Begin on a piece of muslin.

The third way to start a seam is to pin a 3" square of paper or tear-away stabilizer at the beginning of the seam, keeping pins away from the seam line. Begin sewing on the paper, and stitch right onto the fabric, which will feed evenly into the machine. After finishing the seam, carefully pull away the paper or stabilizer.

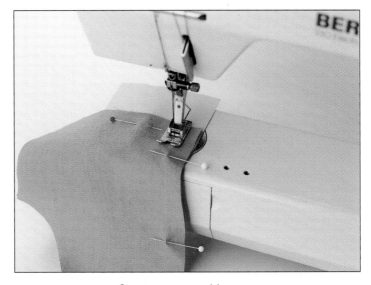

Start a seam with paper.

When beginning or ending a seam, reduce the stitch length. For the first or last 1" to 1-1/2" (2.5 to 3.8cm) of the seam, use 16 to 18 stitches per inch. This methods results in a smooth, strong seam, without having to backstitch.

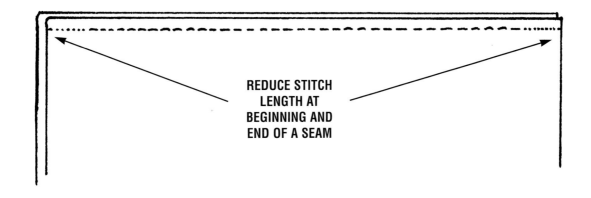

REDUCE STITCH LENGTH AT BEGINNING AND END OF A SEAM

The Serger

The basic serged seam is excellent for lingerie, since the serger takes care of seaming and finishing all in one step. Here are some ideas and suggestions for using your serger:

Tension

When you begin serging, try a test seam and adjust the tension as needed. Write down the settings that work satisfactorily—this provides the information you need to do quick serging, without having to test every time. Some sergers are computerized to automatically adjust the tension to the fabric. Your serger manual guides you through the options available on your serger. The manual has tension guidelines particular to your make and model.

In general, though, the tension is too loose if the threads create a ladder when the seam is pulled apart on the right side. If the seam puckers, the tension is too tight. To correct these problems, turn all the dials back to zero, and then start by setting the tension for the left needle first, then the right needle, then the upper looper, and finally the lower looper.

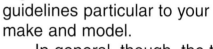

Starting a serged seam.

Starting the Serged Seam

To keep the raw edges accurately lined up at the beginning of a seam, try serging on a small piece of muslin or broadcloth first. Then lift the presser foot, and place the lingerie fabric under the foot, almost touching the muslin, and continue serging on the muslin—and then onto the lingerie fabric. Cut away the muslin when the serged seam is complete.

Types of Seams on the Serger

1. The four thread serged seam is an excellent choice for knit or woven fabric. It produces a strong, stretchy seam, and is smooth in appearance.

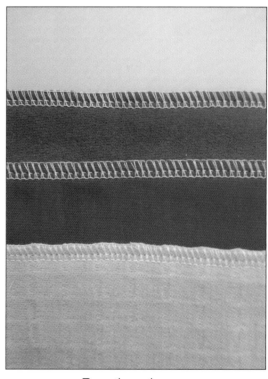

Four thread serge.

2. **The three thread serge** can be used to create a good knit seam, and to finish the raw edges of woven fabrics.

3. **Flatlocking** is a useful serge stitch for joining seams, or for applying lace and elastic. It can also serve as a decorative seam when textured or colored threads are used in the loopers. Flatlocking uses three threads to serge a ladder or trellis on one side of the fabric, and the flatlock seam on the other. Your manual outlines the proper settings and methods for this seam type. The knife of the serger is disengaged for flatlocking.

4. Some sergers have a stitch called the **cover stitch**. The cover stitch stretches. Unlike regular serging, it is sewn on the fabric and not over an edge. Hems, elasticized edges, straps and seams with stretch lace are areas for using the cover stitch. Test your serger settings to establish the best stitch length, tension and differential feed settings.

> ***Tip***: Reinforce at the beginning and the end! To ensure the serged seam ends will not open over the lifetime of the garment, sew a row of short straight stitch (approximately 16 stitches per inch) with the sewing machine at beginning and end of all seams. This stitching line needs to be only 1" (2.5cm) in length.

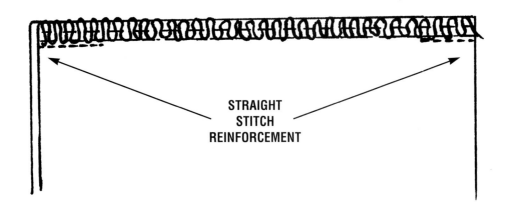

STRAIGHT
STITCH
REINFORCEMENT

Chapter 4

Camisole, Nightie or Slip for Woven Fabric

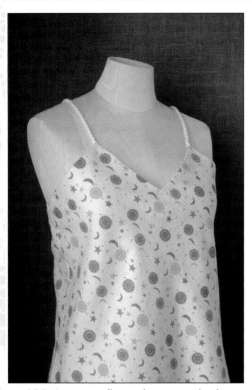

100% cotton flannelette camisole.

100% polyester charmeuse nightie.

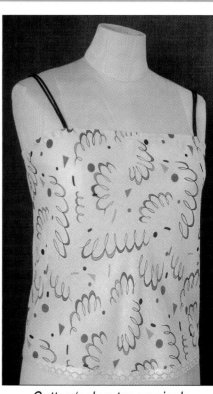

Cotton/polyester camisole.

The nightie and the camisole have been designed for the bias cut of a woven fabric. Bias cut fabrics drape, stretch and move beautifully over the figure, creating an elegant look. There are many wonderful fabrics from which to choose so you can enjoy this design project—and be thrilled with the results. You can choose between the V-neck and straight edge neckline styles. The length of the design also offers great flexibility.

In this chapter you will learn how to draft a simple pattern for a camisole or nightie. Drafting allows you to incorporate your individual measurements into drafting steps, which then lead you in the creation of a pattern. Drafting a pattern may be a new experience for many sewing enthusiasts. The pattern is not the only product of the drafting process. The process also offers the sewer a better understanding of how a pattern works, how clothing fits on our own bodies, and how adjustments can be made to produce our own beautiful result.

Many women find fitting frustrating either because they don't fit into a particular size range, or because they have specific challenges that need to be addressed. Petite, tall, small and large women all have unique fitting requirements. One of the reasons women sew is to satisfy the need for a good fit. This reason is exactly why you should learn how to draft a pattern—to benefit your sewing.

Because bodies are not "standard," we all have variations and differences. Some of the variations we like and others we may not, but at least we have a way to work with what we have! Drafting allows us to create a perfect fit for ourselves.

An excellent idea for checking your draft is to make a test copy, using an inexpensive lining fabric. The test copy is a great tool. It allows you to check the fit, and to see how the design looks—and you are also able to experiment with the sewing. When sewing a test garment, please pay particular attention to the "Fitting Solutions" section at the end of each chapter. When these steps are finished, you will have your own personalized pattern.

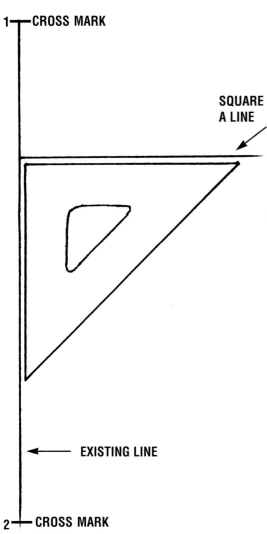

Helpful Definitions

1. A **line** is a straight distance between two points, the length of which is calculated by the drafting directions.

2. Line 0-1 refers to the line running from point 1 to point 2.

3. To **square a line** is to draw a line perpendicular, or at right angles to, an existing line. The drafting square is the most accurate tool to use. Align one edge of the square with the existing line, and draw the line to be squared along the second edge of the drafting square.

4. Parallel lines are two lines that run alongside one another and are always the same distance apart.

5. A **guideline** is a line used in the draft to assist in creating the final shape of the pattern. The guidelines could be drawn as dotted lines, faint pencil lines or colored pencil lines.

6. A **cross mark** is a small hyphen or dash. It is marked across a line, to show the location of a point needed for drafting. For easy reference, mark the number 0,1,2, etc., beside cross marks as you draft and measure the pattern. This labels each cross mark with its own number.

7. Line 0-1 is the bust to waist length. This is an example phrase from the drafting directions. The phrase requires you to draw a line from cross mark 0 to cross mark 1. The length of the line will be known when you measure your body from bust to waist.

8. Line 0-4 is the bust divided by 4 plus 3/8"(1cm) ease.

Note: the calculation in parentheses is completed before the next step in the equation.

This phrase is also from the drafting directions. It explains how to figure out a measurement needed for one of the drafting steps.

Example: Line 0-4 equals (36" bust divided by 4) 9", plus 3/8" ease. So, the length of line 0-4 equals 9-3/8".

Metric example: Line 0-4 equals (92cm bust divided by 4) 23cm plus 1cm ease. So, the length of line 0-4 is 24cm.

Before you begin drafting...

Measure the following areas of the figure with the dressmaker's tape measure:

1. Bust: This is the fullest measurement around the body. Keep the tape measure parallel to the floor.

2. Hip or tummy: Some figures are fullest at the hip line, while others have a round tummy, whose measurement is larger than the hip. Check your own body and record the larger of the two!

3. The length from bust point to waist. Begin at the bust point, measure down the curve of the breast, and then down the rib cage to the waist.

4. The length from the waist to the hip or tummy (the fuller of the two).

5. The length from the waist to the desired garment length (common are mid-thigh and knee-length).

6. A few smaller measurements are also needed. They are explained in the drafting steps.

Drafting the Ladies' Bias Cut Camisole, Nightie or Slip for Woven Fabric

Begin by drawing a long straight line on the left side of drafting paper, and then follow the drafting steps. As you measure to find a particular point, draw a cross mark at the location of the point. Note that the word "hip" is used in the directions, instead of "hip or tummy."

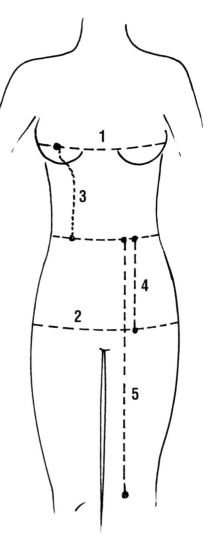

Measure the figure.

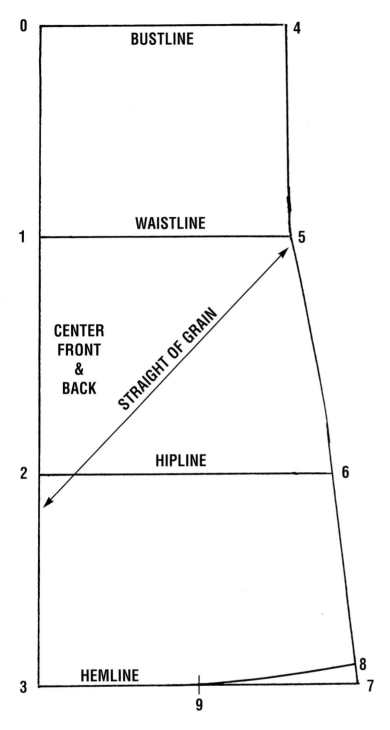

Basic Body of the Camisole, Nightie or Slip for Woven Fabric

1. Line 0-1 is the bust to waist length.

2. Line 1-2 is the waist to hip length.

3. Line 1-3 is the waist to hem length. Label line 0-3 as the center front and center back.

4. Square a line from 0-4. This line equals (bust divided by 4) + 1/2" (1.3cm) ease. Label this as the "bustline."

5. Square a line from 1-5. This is exactly the same as 0-4 from step 4. Label this the "waistline."

6. Square a line from 2-6. This line equals (hip divided by 4) + 3/4" (2cm) ease. Label this as the "hipline."

7. Square a line from 3-7. This line equals (hip divided by 4) + 2-1/2" (6.5cm) ease. Label this as the "hemline."

8. Join points 6 and 7 with a straight line.

9. Join points 4 and 5 with a straight line.

10. Join points 5 and 6 with a long line that curves slightly outward. Note: When drafting this line, look at the overall shape of the side seam from 4 to 5 to 6 to 7. It is easiest to sew, and most attractive on the body, when the side seam shape is a smooth line. Point 6 on the side seam may have a slightly flexible location in order to create the best seam shape.

11. Line 7-8 is 1/4" (.6cm)

12. Line 8-9 is 5" to 6" (12.7cm to 15.4cm). Join points 8 and 9 with a curved line. This slight shaping will create a square corner at 8, and a good hem shape is the final result.

13. Draw a grain line for the bias cutting direction. Line up a drafting square along center front and draw along the 45° angle. Draw this line from edge to edge on the draft.

Jan Bones

33

Front V-Neckline

14. Line 0-11 is the measurement on body from the center front to the strap location you like. Often, the strap is directly above bust point.

15. Line 10-11 is 4" to 6" (10.2cm to 15.4cm). Determine this length by measuring on your body from bust point straight up to desired peak of the nightie, where the strap will start. This measurement allows you to make the level of the neckline attractive for your body. If you are a large size cup, it is particularly helpful.

16. Measure from point 0 to point 12. The distance is 1/4" to 1" (0.6cm to 2.5cm). Join points 10 and 12 with a straight line. This is the V-neck. The angle of the V-neckline works well when it is parallel to the grainline drawn on draft in step 13—that is why there is flexibility in length of line 0-12. When the neckline is on the straight of grain, it will not stretch out of shape.

17. Join point 10 to point 4 with a long, gentle curve.

Straight Front Neckline

18. Measure from point 0 to point 13. The distance is 2" to 3" (5cm-7.5cm).

19. Join point 13 to point 4 with a curved line.

Note: For the easiest sewing, square this line from point 13 for about 1" (2.5cm), and then curve it down to 4.

Back Shaping

20. Measure from point 0 to point 14. The distance is 3" to 4" (7.5cm to 10.2cm).

21. Join point 14 to point 4 with a curved line.

Note: For easiest sewing, square this line at point 14 for about 1" (2.5cm), and then curve it up to 4.

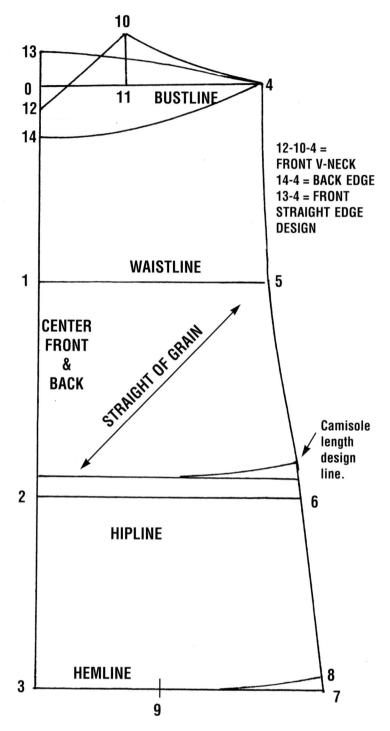

12-10-4 = FRONT V-NECK
14-4 = BACK EDGE
13-4 = FRONT STRAIGHT EDGE DESIGN

Camisole length design line.

Camisole Length Design

The hem of a camisole usually rests above the hip. Select your desired length, and draw the camisole hemline by squaring a line from the center front/back line of the draft. Shape the hem nearest the side seam in same manner as has been described in steps 11 and 12 of the drafting directions (see diagram on page 34).

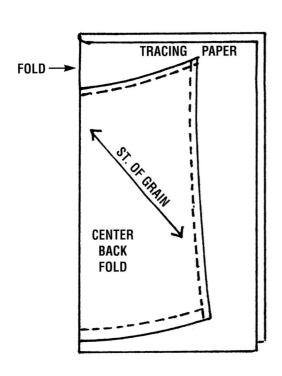

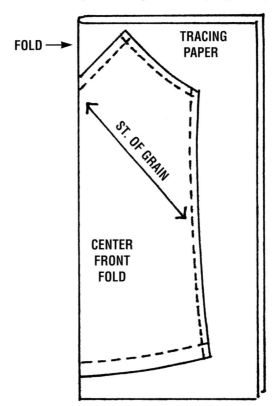

Complete the Pattern

1. In preparation for easier fabric cutting, I recommend tracing a front and back pattern for the camisole or nightie you have drafted. Begin with a folded piece of tissue or tracing paper, and place the fold of the paper along center fold line of the draft. This creates a full width pattern, and will allow for easier, more accurate cutting.

2. When you trace the nightie or camisole, add 5/8" (1.5cm) seam allowances to the sides. Add 3/8" (1cm) seams to the entire front and back top edges and add 3/8" (1cm) for a hem allowance.

3. Draw the straight of grain line on the pattern pieces. Draw it at a 45° angle to the centerline. The longer this line, the simpler the layout on the fabric.

PATTERN
DETAILS

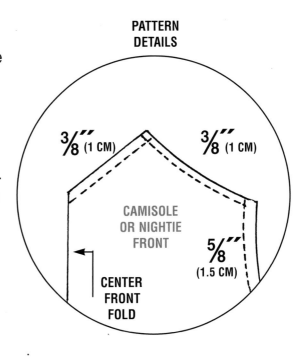

4. A front facing pattern is needed to finish the V-neckline. Begin with a folded piece of tracing paper, and copy the exact shape of the front neckline—including the neckline and side seam allowances mentioned in step 2.

Draw the facing an even width of 2" to 2-1/2" (5cm to 6.5cm). When drawing the lower edge of the facing, make gentle curves for easier sewing later. This lower edge needs a 1/4" (0.6cm) seam allowance. Mark a grainline on the facing, at the same angle as the nightie grainline.

5. The straight front neckline design does not require a facing, as it is finished with elastic.

6. Label the pattern pieces with front, back, front facing, hem edge and any other information you find valuable.

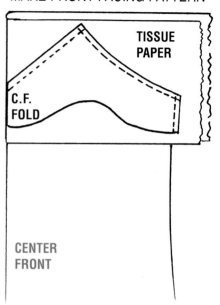

MAKE FRONT FACING PATTERN

Sewing the Camisole or Nightie

Fabric Required

The amount of fabric varies according to the figure's size and the length you choose to make your design. The following guidelines will get you started:

Camisole: 3/4 yard of 45" to 60" width (0.7M of 115cm to 150 cm width)

Nightie: 1-3/4 yard of 45" to 60" width (1.6M of 115cm to 150cm width)

Layout

Spread the single layer of fabric onto cutting surface. It is very important not to allow any fabric to hang over the edge, so fold up any extra to keep all fabric on the flat surface. The placement of the grainline is of the utmost importance for the success of the garment, and hanging fabric could cause shifting or pulling.

V-Neck Design: Cut 1 front, 1 back and 1 facing

Straight Edge Design: Cut 1 front and 1 back

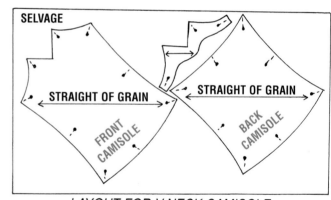

LAYOUT FOR V-NECK CAMISOLE

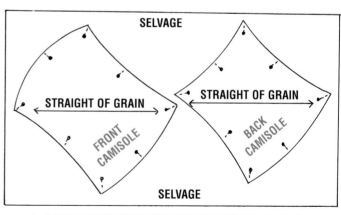

LAYOUT FOR STRAIGHT NECK EDGE DESIGN

Sewing Instructions

1. Sew the side seams. The seams are 5/8" (1.5cm). The French seam, as explained below, creates a beautiful finish for the bias cut seam:

Place the two side seam edges wrong sides together, and sew a 1/4" (.6cm) seam. Press the seams to the back, being careful to not stretch the bias cut fabric pieces.

Refold the same side seam edges, and now place them right sides together. Sew a 3/8" (1cm) seam. Press the seam allowances toward the back of the garment, and the seam is complete.

French seam on bias cut cotton.

Finished French seam on camisole.

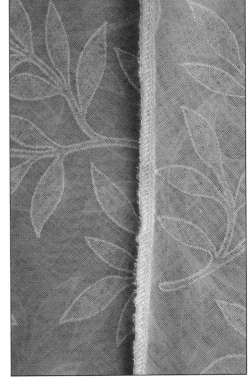

If you prefer to use a serger, line the fabric up so the extra seam allowance will be trimmed during stitching.

Serged seam on bias cut cotton.

Jan Bones

2. Decide on your straps. You might use ribbon or adjustable straps, or make your own from matching fabric. To make 1/2" (1.3cm) wide fabric straps follow these steps (Note—these are open ended straps, meaning both ends will be finished when sewn to the camisole):

❖ Cut two pieces of fabric along lengthwise grain of fabric, 1-1/2" (3.8cm) wide and 14" to 17" (35.5cm to 43cm) long.

❖ Fold each fabric strap in half with right sides together. Sew a 1/4" (.6cm) seam. Press one seam allowance open.

❖ Turn the tube right side out. A wire loop turner is a simple but effective tool to use for turning the strap. A bobby pin also works well. Cut a small snip in the fold of the tube to give either tool a bit of fabric to hold while you turn the tube right side out.

❖ Press the strap to line up the seam along one edge of the tube.

❖ Topstitch along each edge of the strap, if desired.

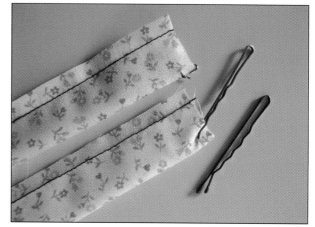

Turn the strap with a loop turner or a bobby pin.

Tip: **Finished straps can be 1/4" to 2" (.6cm to 5cm) in width. To calculate the required amount of fabric to cut, multiply the desired finished width by 2 and add 1/2" (1.3cm). The extra 1/2" (1.3cm) allows for a 1/4" (.6cm) seam.**

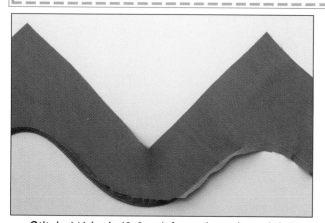

Stitch 1/4 inch (0.6cm) from the edge of the facing and press up the raw edge.

Topstitch the edge of the facing.

3. Finish the V-neckline with the facing:

❖ The curved lower edge of the facing may be finished by serging with a three thread stitch. This is a quick, neat technique.

❖ The curved lower edge may also be finished in the following way:

❖ First, straight stitch a line 1/4" (.6cm) from the raw edge, using 11 to12 stitches per inch.

❖ Press along the stitching line, so that 1/4" (0.6cm) of fabric goes to the wrong side.

❖ Topstitch 1/8" (.3cm) from the fold. Press lightly.

Lay the straps to the right side of the camisole.

Pin the facing, camisole, and straps together.

Sew the layers together.

Lay the straps on the right side of nightie, at the top of the peak. Place the facing right sides together with the front—the straps should be in between—and pin. Fold and pin the 5/8" (1.5cm) side seam of facing to the wrong side.

Sew from one side seam, up and down the V-neck areas to the other side seam with a 3/8" (1cm) allowance. Sew across the area where the straps are located, and then continue down the V-neck.

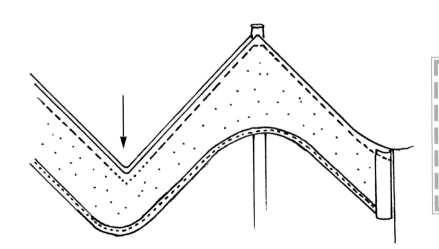

REDUCE STITCH LENGTH AT POINT OF V NECKLINE

Tip: I like to reduce the stitch length for about 1″ (2.5cm) on each side of the V-neck's point to reinforce it well.

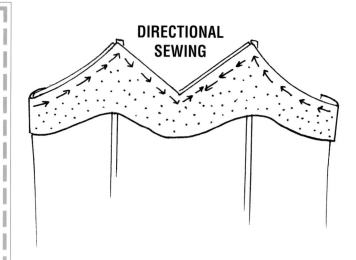

DIRECTIONAL SEWING

Tip: For V-neck shapes, "directional sewing" may be a good choice. Directional sewing means that you would sew from the side seam, up and down the peak, and pivot at center front and sew for 1/2" (1.3cm). Then start at the other side seam and sew to meet the stitching near the center front. This technique makes the two sides of the neckline appear equal, because they are sewn in the same direction. This is a good technique to employ in many areas of all sewing projects.

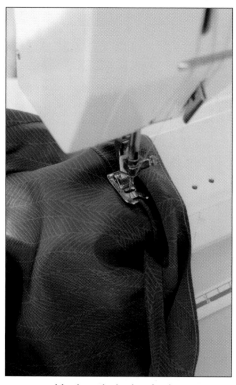

Understitch the facing.

Press the facing.

The V is secure because of the stitching technique—so clip it well into the stitching, and turn the facing to the inside. The straps will pull away from the nightie, neatly finished and sewn into place.

Understitch and/or topstitch to keep the facing to the inside of the nightie. Understitching is a line of straight sewing, 1/8" (.3cm) from the seam line, catching only facing and seam allowances. Parts of the neckline are very hard to reach when understitching, so just sew as much as is possible. The facing will now lie smoothly on the inside of the camisole. Press the facing along the neckline edge.

4. The back of nightie is finished with 3/8" (1cm) elastic. The raw edge will not fray because of the bias cutting; therefore, the zigzag used to sew the elastic could be a simple finish. (Note: If you have a serger, you might serge the raw edge of the nightie back with a three thread serging.) The elastic needs to be approximately the same length as the distance between the side seam locations on your body. Measure your body and/or try the elastic on. This makes the elastic about 1" to 3" (2.5cm to 7.5cm) shorter than the actual nightie. Vary the amount depending on your fitting preference. Mark both the elastic and the nightie edge into quarters, and then:

Sew elastic to the back edge of the camisole.

❖ Pin the elastic to the wrong side of nightie, matching the pins.

❖ Sew on the lower edge of the elastic, using a medium width zigzag.

❖ Turn the elastic to the wrong side and stitch along the lower edge. This row of stitching will show on the right side of the fabric.

If you prefer some adjustment in the back, make a casing by sewing the 3/8" (1cm) seam to the nightie back, and run 1/4" (0.6cm) elastic through the opening.

Pin, and hand or machine stitch the facing to the side seams.

5. Finish the straight front nightie or camisole with elastic around the entire top edge, front and back. This technique is quick and allows you to create a personalized fit by varying the amount of elastic sewn to the garment.

Turn the elastic and sew the second row. Pin and sew the facing to the side seam.

❖ Fit a length of elastic around your figure, above the bust. Cut the correct length of 3/8" (1cm) wide elastic.

❖ Sew the elastic into a circle.

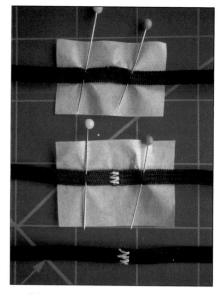

Tip: I like to put the ends of elastic together without overlapping, as it is less bulky. Pin the ends of the elastic to a piece of paper or tear-away stabilizer. This gives you something to hold onto when stitching. Zigzag to join the ends of the elastic, and pull off the paper or stabilizer.

Pin the elastic to paper, and zigzag together.

❖ Mark the circle of elastic and nightie into quarters with pins or chalk.

❖ Follow the directions in step 4 for sewing elastic, using a plain or multiple zigzag.

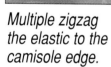

Multiple zigzag the elastic to the camisole edge.

Plain zigzag the elastic to the camisole edge.

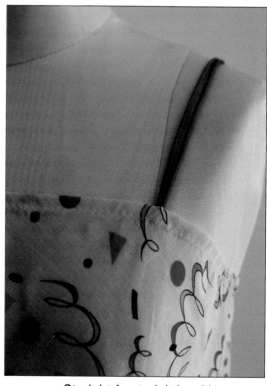

Straight front nightie with velvet cord straps.

6. For the straight front neckline nightie or camisole, you can also finish the top edge with stretch lace, instead of elastic. This has the same advantages as elastic, and also provides a decorative finish.

Fit the stretch lace around your body, above your bust. Cut the correct length, plus 3/8" (1cm) for joining.

The bias edge will not fray, but as an option, you could serge the edge. The zigzag used to sew the stretch lace will also serve as a neat finish. Use the quartering technique, and lap the stretch lace onto the edge of the right side of the nightie. Stitch.

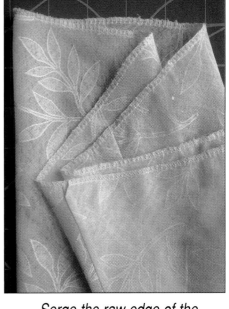

Serge the raw edge of the bias cut camisole.

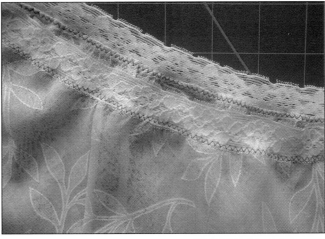

Sew elastic stretch lace to the straight neckline camisole.

7. Try on the nightie, checking the length and placement of the straps.

The straps should be 4" to 5" (10.2cm to 12.7cm) on each side of center back.

For the straight front neckline, the straps should be 5" to 6" (12.7cm to 15cm) from the center front.

Check strap placement.

8. Complete the hem. Try a sample hem, to test for accurate stitch length and appearance. Here are a few of my suggestions:

❖ Turn the hem to the wrong side, and stitch with a twin needle, or multiple zigzag. To keep the fabric from stretching, hold your finger behind the presser foot, on the throat plate of the sewing machine. Then, as you sew, allow the fabric to "pile up" a little at a time. The resulting hem will lie smooth after a light pressing with the iron.

Rolled hem on a bias cut edge.

❖ Use the rolled hem foot on your sewing machine. Help the presser foot by folding in 1/8" (.3cm) of hem edge to the wrong side, and then roll this fold into the foot. Practice using this foot. Once you master this skill, you will be able to produce beautiful, professional-looking finishes. The rolled hem foot cannot sew over the side seam allowances—the solution is to avoid it! Starting 1-1/2" (3.8cm) away from the side seam, sew across the front of the hem. Stop 1-1/2" (3.8cm) from the other side seam, and trim the threads. Follow same procedure for back.

Then, replace the regular foot on the sewing machine, and stitch the few inches over each side seam following the same roll as the rest of the hem. A little pinning helps at the seam junction.

❖ Serge the raw edge, turn and topstitch.

❖ Lap the lace onto the hem edge, and multiple zigzag the two layers together. Use a medium width zigzag for narrow lace. Either elastic stretch lace or regular lingerie lace may be used.

Finish a hem with lace.

Fitting Solutions

Problem #1: The straps tend to slide off your shoulders.

Solution: Try moving them closer to the center back. The increased angle helps to keep the straps up on your shoulders.

Problem #2: The fabric gaps at the side of the breast.

Solution: If the figure has a very round breast, or a large cup size, the bias of the fabric may not have enough ease to create a pleasing, smooth shape. The best solution is to pin a dart into the fabric of the nightie test copy. Then, transfer the dart markings to your pattern, so you will have the fitting solved for future sewing. The shape of the facing also needs to be changed, to reflect the shape of the pattern after the dart is folded. Fold the dart in the pattern, and then trace a new facing.

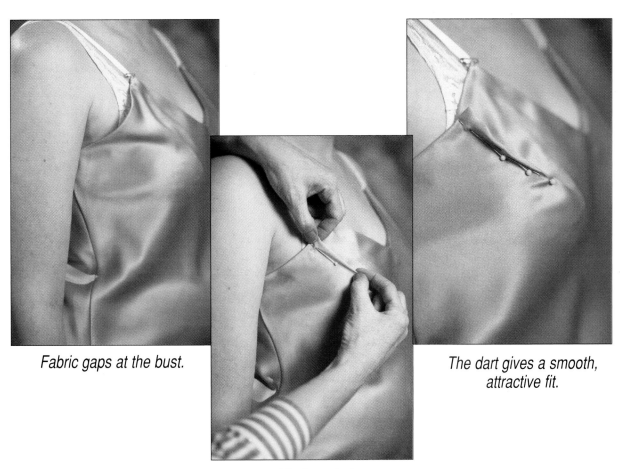

Fabric gaps at the bust.

Pin in a dart.

The dart gives a smooth, attractive fit.

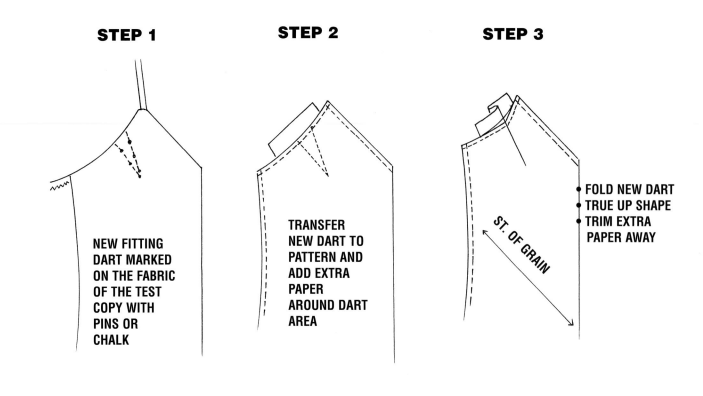

STEP 1

NEW FITTING DART MARKED ON THE FABRIC OF THE TEST COPY WITH PINS OR CHALK

STEP 2

TRANSFER NEW DART TO PATTERN AND ADD EXTRA PAPER AROUND DART AREA

STEP 3

ST. OF GRAIN

• FOLD NEW DART
• TRUE UP SHAPE
• TRIM EXTRA PAPER AWAY

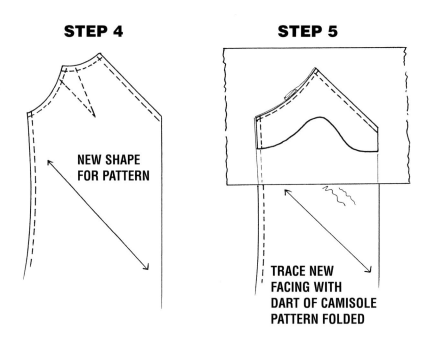

STEP 4

NEW SHAPE FOR PATTERN

STEP 5

TRACE NEW FACING WITH DART OF CAMISOLE PATTERN FOLDED

Problem #3: The front V-neckline seems to rest too low or too high.

Solution: The distance measured on your draft from point 0 to point 12 determines the neckline level. Also check the location of point 10. Does it need to be moved up or down? Change the measurements and the draft to better suit your personal taste.

Problem #4: You feel too naked, or too well-covered—you want your breast covered with more or less fabric in the area above bust point.

Solution: This is the perfect opportunity to check the measurements you used for drafting. The distance from point 10 to point 11 on the drafted pattern matches the measurement on the body described in step 15 of the drafting directions. This area of your design may need some alteration to suit the level of neckline that you find comfortable.

Plus-sized women and women who wear a generous bra cup size will find this a common fitting detail to check. For all figure types, if the distance from shoulder to breast is long, the distance from point 10 to 11 may need adjustment—and often the needed adjustment is to make the distance longer.

Variations

1. A long nightie is possible in a bias cut. The secret is in the cutting. The width of most cottons will only allow the bias cut nightie to be knee-length or shorter. The solution is to add a seam. The seam must be on the straight of grain, so that it blends well.

Plan your placement of your pattern on the fabric, to determine where the extra fabric is needed.

Sew an extra piece of fabric onto the main section of fabric, to allow the placement of the entire nightie pattern. Use a small seam allowance to join the two layers, to keep the seam inconspicuous. Then, cut and sew the nightie. This method has been used for centuries, when pattern pieces are longer or wider than an available fabric.

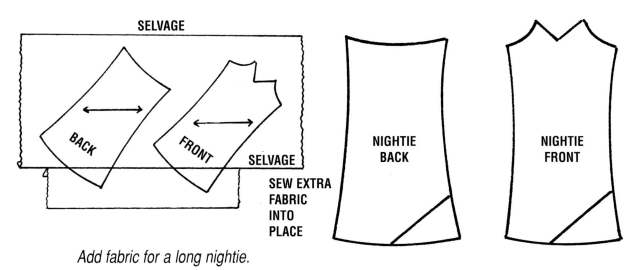

Add fabric for a long nightie.

Fabric pieces after cutting.

2. Partly sheer fabrics are great choices for sexy and elegant lingerie. Consider cutting the neckline facing in a different fabric from the nightie. Try using a sheer fabric like organdy (polyester or silk), organza (cotton) or voile (cotton or polyester/cotton). These fabrics enhance the look of the neckline, as they are almost invisible. Sew the camisole or nightie in the same manner described in the sewing steps.

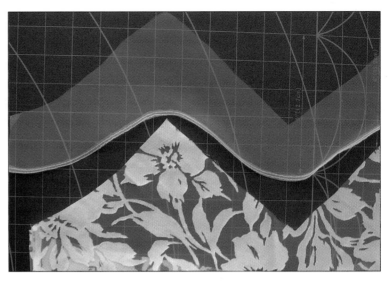

Use sheer fabric for the neckline facing.

Double-layer chiffon makes a lovely nightie.

3. For another way to use sheer fabric, double the entire camisole or nightie. Chiffon, voile and other soft, sheer fabrics are great choices for this design idea. Cut two fronts and two backs. Sew one front to one back at the side seams. Repeat this process for the second front and back you have cut. Then, put the two camisoles right sides together. Sew the front neckline—treat the second front just like a facing, and understitch it. Finish the back edge with elastic. Hem the two layers separately. Here, you can have a little fun with the possibilities—different colored layers, dark and iridescent layers, a print layer and a plain layer...let your imagination go wild!

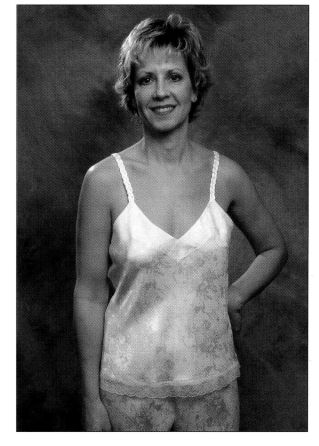

Add lace along the facing line.   *Add braided straps of self fabric.*

4. Braided straps are made of the same fabric as the camisole or nightie. Cut six strips of fabric on the lengthwise grain. Make the tubes, and then sew two sets of three strips together at one end. Braid and sew the completed strap into the design.

5. You can also draft this design for the pre-teen figure or the developing figure. The great feature of the bias cutting direction is that it takes on the shape of the body. This is an excellent opportunity to sew something special for a smaller, slender body. Select fabrics with some weight, like flannelette, or a textured woven fabric, such as polyester jacquard.

> **Tip:** As you try different lingerie designs and patterns, keep track of your measurements, your weight and the date you made a particular pattern and garment. Pin a sample of the fabric you use to your pattern for future reference. Note pattern changes, sewing ideas and details to remember for the next time.
>
> To organize your patterns, punch holes in 8-1/2" x 11" (21.5cm x 28cm) envelopes and store them in a three ring binder. Each envelope holds a pattern, a sample garment if you choose to keep it, and any written information you need. All of these details combine to make your patterns easy to use again and again.

Chapter 5

Camisole, Nightie or Full Slip for Knit Fabric

Combine soft gathers at the bust, V-neck shaping and a gentle A-line silhouette, and you have a design that is sure to be a favorite. All the pattern pieces are included in this chapter. The camisole design has a front bodice section with the seam under the bust. When worn under clothing, the camisole gives a smooth, attractive fit, as the gathers create shaping. Instructions for lengthening the skirt section of the pattern to a knee-length nightie or full slip are included as well.

Knit fabrics such as cotton single knit and nylon tricot are excellent choices. Polyester interlock, stretch laces and two way stretch fabric would be suitable as well. Or, use a combination of fabrics, and make the bodice different from the skirt. The only notions required are:

❖ Thread;

❖ 1/4"(.6cm) wide lingerie elastic; and

❖ 4"(10.2cm) piece of 1/8" (.3cm) satin ribbon.

❖ Lace is optional for the hemline, and also for the neck edge.

Select the size of the pattern, according to your bust measurement. You have the option of using a bodice pattern for an A to B cup , or one that is for the C cup. Use the following chart of measurements to help in size selection. Many figures require different sizes for the top and the bottom. For this reason, hip measurements are also listed. Take advantage of the multisize pattern—if you measure one size in the bust area and another size in the hip, trace the two sizes that work for you and your body proportions. A French curve or ruler will help you to draw continuous, smooth lines.

Bust	32"-33" (81-84cm)	34"-35" (86-89cm)	36"-38" (91-96cm)	39"- 41" (99-104cm)	42"-44" (107-112cm)
Hip	34"-35" (86-89cm)	36"-37" (91-94cm)	38"-40" (96-101cm)	41"-43" (104-109cm)	44"-46" (112-117cm)

> ***Tip:*** When designing the pattern size range for this book, paper size had to be taken into account. The pattern pieces, when they are in full scale, fit onto the largest size of photocopier paper that is widely available, an 11" x 17" (28cm x 43cm) sheet. To increase the range, you could draw more sizes by observing the changes in the shaping between the sizes, and following the additions and subtractions in fullness throughout the pattern pieces.

The grid drawing of the camisole pattern is included here in half scale. Seam allowances of 3/8" (1cm) are included in the pattern, and the elastic used can be 1/4" (0.6cm) or 3/8" (1cm). There are two ways to make the full scale pattern for sewing:

1. Use a photocopier: Set the copier to x200, place this book into the machine and make a copy of each of the three pattern grids. You will produce a bodice front, the back band, the strap and the front/back skirt. The enlarged patterns will fit onto 11" x 17" (28cm x 43cm) paper. The pattern has grain lines and fold lines and is ready for layout and cutting.

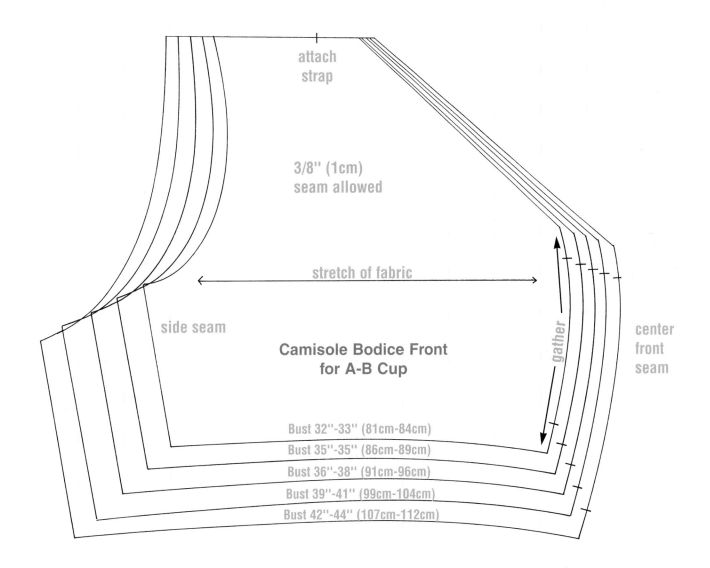

attach strap

3/8" (1cm) seam allowed

stretch of fabric

side seam

gather

center front seam

Camisole Bodice Front for A-B Cup

Bust 32"-33" (81cm-84cm)
Bust 35"-35" (86cm-89cm)
Bust 36"-38" (91cm-96cm)
Bust 39"-41" (99cm-104cm)
Bust 42"-44" (107cm-112cm)

2. Draw the pattern onto 1" (2.5cm) grid paper. One square on the grid equals 1" (2.5cm). Count out the squares to draw the basic shape of the pattern first and then draw curves and shapes using a curved ruler, along with the grid, as your guide.

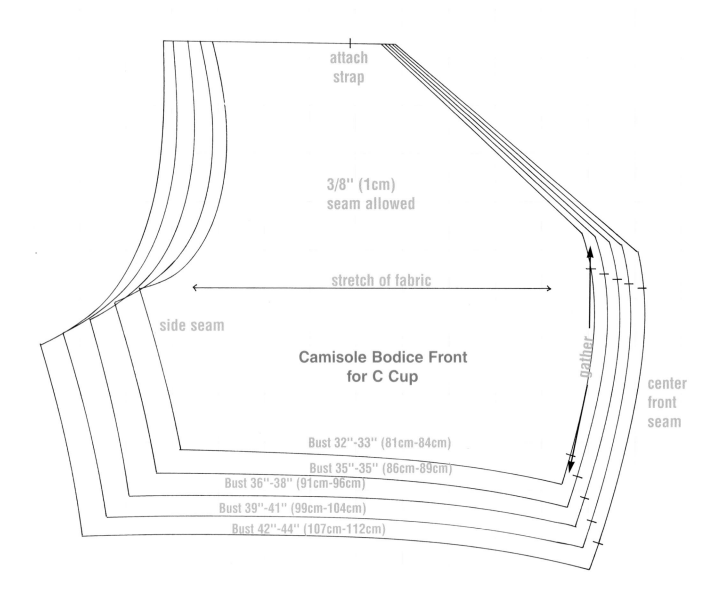

attach strap

3/8" (1cm) seam allowed

stretch of fabric

side seam

Camisole Bodice Front for C Cup

gather

center front seam

Bust 32"-33" (81cm-84cm)
Bust 35"-35" (86cm-89cm)
Bust 36"-38" (91cm-96cm)
Bust 39"-41" (99cm-104cm)
Bust 42"-44" (107cm-112cm)

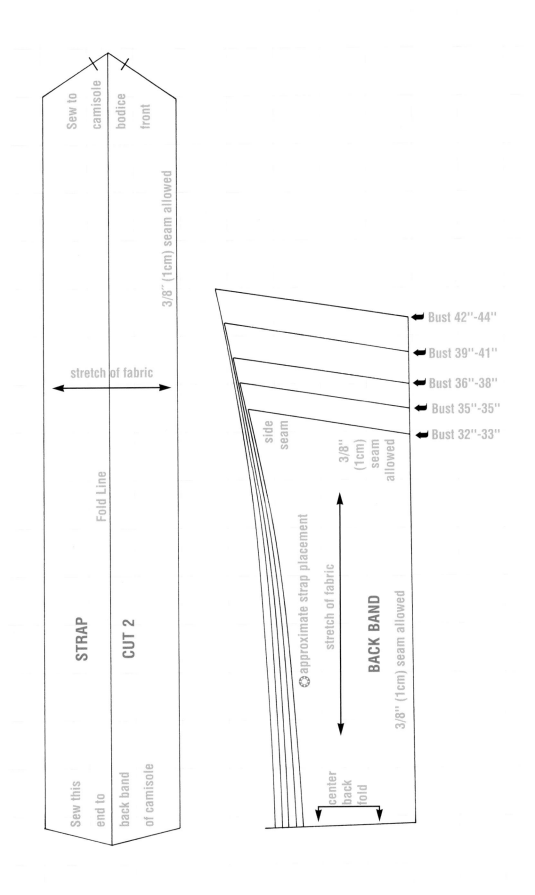

STRAP

CUT 2

Sew to camisole bodice front

3/8" (1cm) seam allowed

stretch of fabric

Fold Line

Sew this end to back band of camisole

Bust 42"-44"
Bust 39"-41"
Bust 36"-38"
Bust 35"-35"
Bust 32"-33"

side seam

✿ approximate strap placement

3/8" (1cm) seam allowed

stretch of fabric

BACK BAND

3/8" (1cm) seam allowed

center back fold

Jan Bones

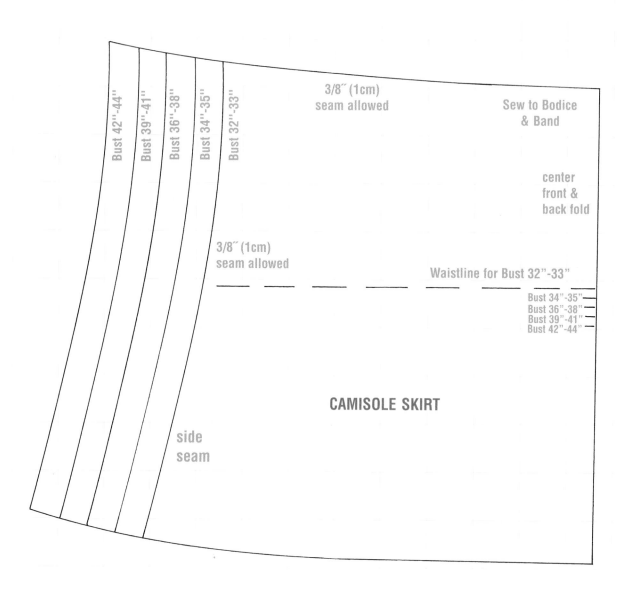

Bust 42"-44"

Bust 39"-41"

Bust 36"-38"

Bust 34"-35"

Bust 32"-33"

3/8″ (1cm)
seam allowed

Sew to Bodice
& Band

center
front &
back fold

3/8″ (1cm)
seam allowed

Waistline for Bust 32"-33"

Bust 34"-35"
Bust 36"-38"
Bust 39"-41"
Bust 42"-44"

CAMISOLE SKIRT

side
seam

Fabric Required

Camisole: 3/4 yard (0.7M) of 60" (150cm) width
Knee-Length Nightie: 1-1/4 yard (1.2M) of 60" (150cm) width

Layout—cut the following:

2 front bodices
1 back band on fold
1 front skirt on fold
1 back skirt on fold
2 straps

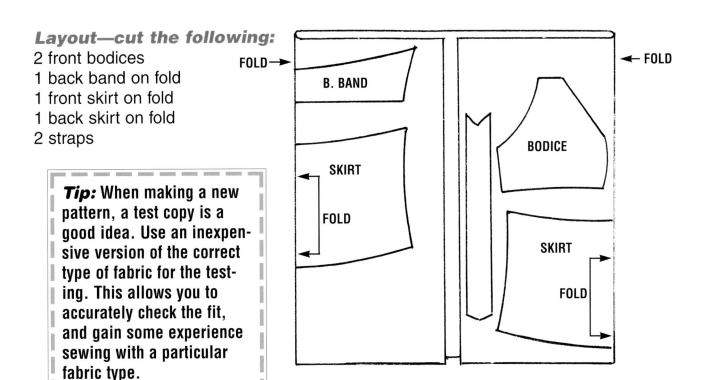

Tip: When making a new pattern, a test copy is a good idea. Use an inexpensive version of the correct type of fabric for the testing. This allows you to accurately check the fit, and gain some experience sewing with a particular fabric type.

Detailed Sewing Order

1. Finish the V-neck edge with 1/4" (.6cm) or 3/8" (1cm) elastic.
a). Lay the elastic on the wrong side. To reduce bulk, stop the elastic 1/2" (1.3cm) from the top and the bottom of the V-neck.
b). Stitch on the inner edge of the elastic with a medium width zigzag.
c). Turn the elastic to the wrong side and stitch again.
2. Using a scant 3/8" (1cm) seam, sew a line of gathering along the center front on each of the two bodice sections, and pull the threads until the edge measures:
3" (7.5cm) for bust sizes 32"-33" and 34"-35"
3 1/2" (9cm) for bust sizes 36"-38" and 39"-41"
4" (10.2cm) for bust size 42"-44"

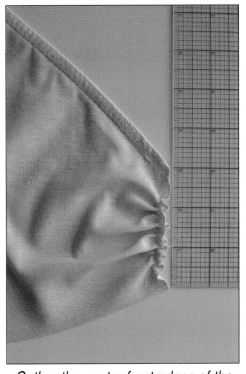

Gather the center front edges of the bodice pieces.

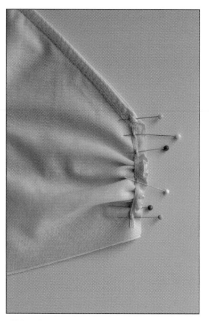

Pin the two bodices together at the center front.

Sew the center seam.

View from the right side of the camisole.

3. Pin the two bodices, right sides together, at the center front. Move the gathers around so they are even. To prevent this gathered edge from stretching, use a piece of 1/8" (.3cm) wide satin ribbon, stitching it in as you sew the seam.
4. Sew the side seams of the front bodice and the back band with the right sides together, using a 3/8" (1cm) seam. Press the seams to the front.

5. Sew the side seams of the skirt front and back using a 3/8" (1cm) seam. Press these seams toward back.
6. Sew under the bust seam to join the bodice to the skirt, taking care to line up the side seams perfectly.

Tip: Reduce bulk at the side seam by pressing the bodice seams to the front, and the skirt seams to the back, thereby staggering the seams.

Sew all side seams and the under bust seam.

7. This is a good time to carefully try on the camisole or nightie.

8. Pin 1/4" or 3/8" (0.6cm or 1cm) elastic to the wrong side of the back and underarm areas of the camisole. Along the underarm areas, make the elastic the same length as the fabric edge. Across the back band, make the elastic 1" to 2" (2.5cm to 5cm) shorter than the width of the fabric.

> ***Tip:*** Try testing the length of elastic on your body first. To reduce bulk, stop the elastic 1/2" (1.3cm) from the top corners of bodice. Sew the elastic into place with only one row of zigzag at this time.

Sew elastic to the back edge.

9. Make the two straps. Place the right sides together, sew, turn and press. These are open-ended straps; they will be finished when they are attached to the camisole.

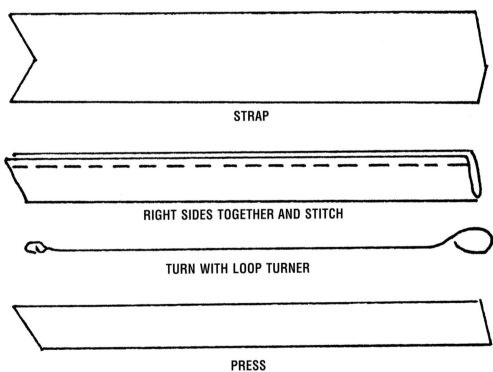

STRAP

RIGHT SIDES TOGETHER AND STITCH

TURN WITH LOOP TURNER

PRESS

> ***Tip:*** When sewing straps, I like to use a narrow zigzag to add stretch and strength.

10. Sew a line of gathering along the top of the bodice. Pull the threads until the edge measures 1-1/4" (3.2cm)—for all sizes. (Option: Fold in a couple of small pleats instead of gathering the edge.)

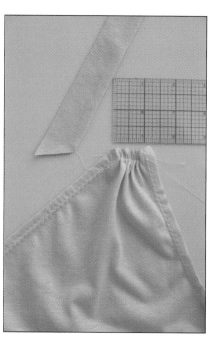

Pin the strap to the bodice.

11. Pin the strap to the right side of the top of the bodice by matching the single notches. Wrap 1/4" (0.6cm) allowance on the underarm side of the bodice over the elastic. Stitch all the layers with a 3/8" (1cm) seam.

Gather the top edge of the bodice.

12. Pull the strap away from the bodice. This folds the elastic to the inside of the bodice, making it ready for second row of zigzag. To hold the strap seams into place, topstitch through all the layers.

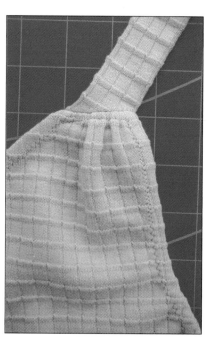

Pull the strap up.

Sew the second row of zigzag, and topstitch.

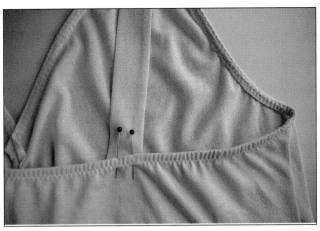

Position the straps.

13. Fit the camisole, and position the straps approximately 3" to 4" (7.6cm-10.2cm) on each side of the center back. Check the strap length, and stitch.

14. Hem the lower edge of camisole. Choose one of the following finishes:

❖ Lap the lace onto the hem edge, and multiple zigzag the two layers together. Use a medium width zigzag for narrow lace. Elastic stretch lace or regular lingerie lace may also be used.

Tip: Carefully trim away excess fabric. This may be particularly necessary if the lace is scalloped and fabric shows between the curves.

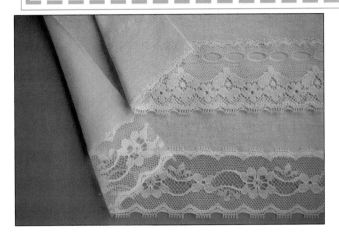

Sew lace to the hem.

Hem the nightie and then add lace, or sew stretch lace on the hem.

❖ Serge the raw edge, turn and topstitch. The turned hem finish gives weight to the bottom edge, and it is a durable finish. Press 3/4" to 1" (2 to 2.5cm) to the wrong side, and stitch a multiple zigzag along edge of hem. This is a good stitch because it lies smoothly and has stretch, and it prevents the edge of fabric from curling.

❖ The twin needle is another option. It makes a very attractive, stretchy, professional look. This is achieved by sewing from right side of fabric. After sewing the hem with a twin needle, turn to the wrong side of the camisole and trim away the extra fabric above the stitching.

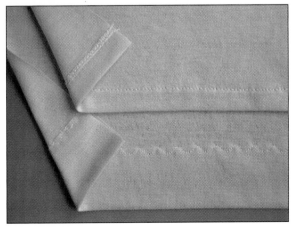

Serge, turn and straight stitch.

Fitting Solutions

Problem #1: You would like a better fit over the bust. Different amounts of stretch in the fabric, different breast shapes, and personal choice all play a part in this fitting area. Fabric with more stretch creates a different fit from that of firmer fabrics.

Solution #1: Take in the side seam if you feel there is too much fabric over the bust. Make a note on the pattern of the change, and the fabric used. If a particular fabric and its stretch fit you well, make a note on your pattern and keep a fabric sample.

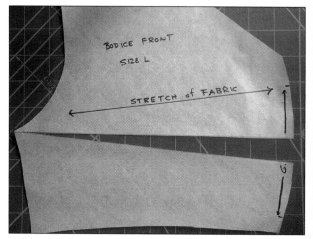

Cut and spread the pattern.

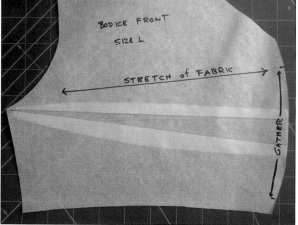

Add extra paper— now, the pattern has more area to gather.

Solution #2: If more fabric is needed to fit over the breast area, you can cut it and spread the cut edges apart to adjust the pattern. Spread the pattern apart on the center front line, and allow the side seam to remain the original length. The extra fabric creates more gathers, and a better fit for a fuller bust. If less fabric is wanted for a small bust, cut the pattern and lap it to make it smaller.

Problem #2: The V-neck sits away from the body.

Solution: When the elastic was sewn to the neckline, it was the same length as the neckline. To change this, make the elastic slightly smaller then the edge of the neckline, so that it pulls the neckline in toward the body and lies smoothly.

> **Tip:** "Directional Sewing" may also be a solution. When sewing a V-neck, the direction of the sewing should be from the center front up toward the shoulder on both bodice pieces.

Problem #3: When you check the appearance of the nightie back, you notice that it lifts up, or it hangs down, away from your body.

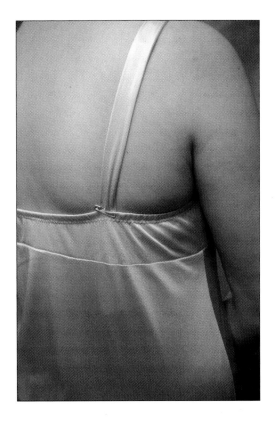

Straps are not in the correct position; nor are they the correct length.

Corrected fit of the camisole.

Solution: For the nightie to rest attractively across your back, the straps need to be the correct length. If the nightie lifts, try lengthening the straps to correct the problem. If the edge of the nightie hangs away from the body, the amount of elastic across the back edge may need to be shortened, and/or the straps may require shortening.

Problem # 5: You do not like the way the skirt of the camisole lies over your body. It feels too tight or too loose.

Solution: The fit of the camisole in this area is important. Too much fabric appears as wrinkles under clothing, and not enough fabric can cause the camisole to creep up your body. Try the camisole on your body and check the ease. Decide whether you would like to take in the side seams slightly. If it is too snug, note on your pattern the extra fabric needed for the next time you sew the camisole.

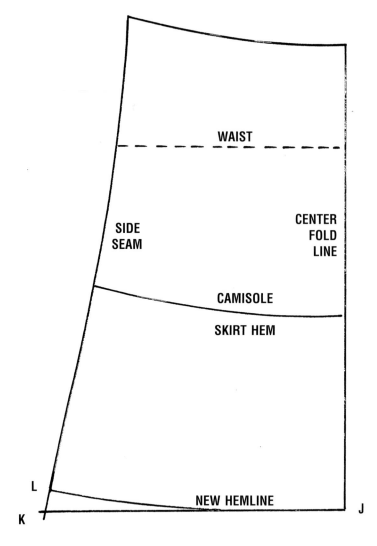

Variations

1. Lengthen the pattern for a nightie or full length slip design:

Trace the camisole skirt onto pattern paper, allowing sufficient length below the tracing for your new design. For example, you may want a knee length nightie—an average waist to knee measurement is 24" (60cm). Mark the waistline indicated on the cami-sole skirt pattern, and square a line over to the side seam.

The side seam and center line must be lengthened. Place your ruler along camisole skirt side seam and continue to draw the line down to the area of your desired length. Place your ruler along the camisole skirt center line and continue drawing the line down. Mark a "J" at end of this line.

Square a line from J, and draw until it crosses the side seam line. Label the junction "K."

Some shaping at K creates an attractive hem. Along the center line, measure the length from the camisole hemline to the new hemline. Measure this same length down the side seam, from the camisole hemline, and mark an "L."
Draw a long gentle curve from L to the hem. The curved line should be about 6" to 8" (15.4cm to 20.4cm) long, and L should be a square corner. This makes a nice shape at the hem and side seam corner when the front and back are sewn together.

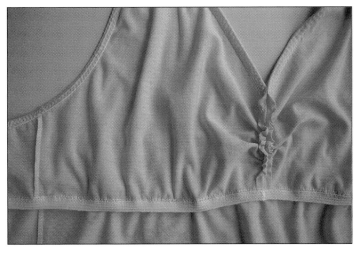
Staggered seam reduces bulk.

2. To achieve a closer fit and more support under the bust, sew elastic to the under-bust seam allowance. "Plush back" elastic would be an excellent choice. Use any width from 1/4" to 1"(.6cm to 2.5cm) elastic (wider elastic gives more support) and try the length around your body to determine the best amount. With a zigzag, sew the ends of the elastic together into a circle. Mark the circle into quarters and pin it to the seam, so that the elastic touches the skin. Sew along the top edge of the elastic with a zigzag, and attach it to the seam allowances.

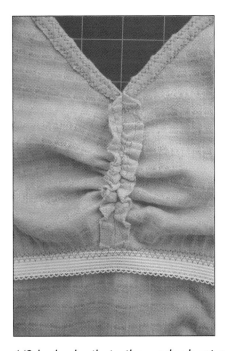
Sew 1/2-inch elastic to the under bust seam.

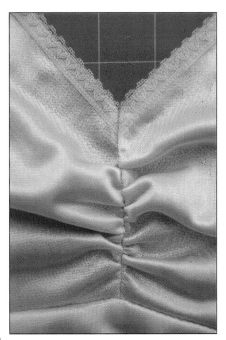
Sew narrow lace to the V-neckline.

3. Finish the neckline with lace. Trim off the 1/4"(.6cm) allowance from the V-neck edge of the bodice. Pin the lace to the V-neck edge and sew on both edges of the lace with a multiple zigzag.

4. A ruffle, sometimes called a flounce, can be added to the lower edge of the nightie. The secret to ruffles is that they must not look too skimpy or too full. A simple guideline is to measure around the edge of the hemline. Multiply this measurement by 2 or 2-1/2 or 3 to give the length of the ruffle needed. Of course, the amount of fabric you have might help you decide how much fullness is possible! Sew the sections together to make the entire ruffle. I like marking the nightie hem and ruffle into quarters or eighths, so I know the fabric will be equally distributed.

Chapter 6

Half Slips

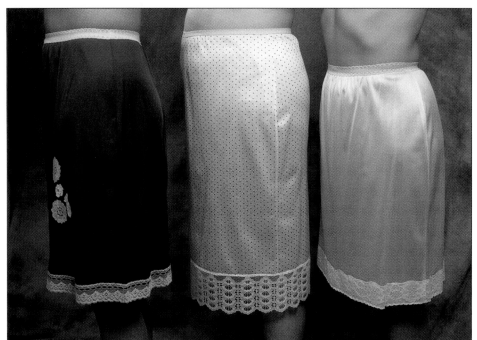

Three half slips.

A timeless lingerie design, the half slip is great to wear with unlined clothing. It allows skirts and dresses to hang gracefully over the body without clinging. Sizing is really very important with this design. Petite and tall women require the length of a slip to be adjusted for their body proportions. Plus-sized figures benefit from a great-fitting slip to ensure comfort and elegance in the drape of their clothing.

The fabric most commonly used to create slips is nylon tricot. Anti-static Antron® nylon is truly great. Polyester interlock or other lightweight, slippery fabrics are also suitable for slips. Beautiful lace trims might be used with the slip fabrics to add elegance.

In this chapter, you will learn to design a variety of half slips:

A half slip may be designed from a commercial pattern for a straight skirt. This is an excellent—and quick—method for designing a slip that fits perfectly under a skirt you already have!

Your own personalized half slip may be drafted from your body measurements. Straight cut and A-line styles are described.

Drafting steps are also included for the wonderful 6-panel slip with godets. This elegant slip is a classic favorite because of its femininity and grace.

In the "Variations" section at the end of the chapter, the bias cut half slip is described. The advantage with this slip is the range of possibilities for variety. There are many woven fabrics from which to choose; cottons, rayons, polyesters and silks. Make this slip in the same fabric as the woven camisole in Chapter 4 for an elegant lingerie set.

Design a Half Slip from a Commercial Pattern

The pattern for a half slip can be made from any regular straight skirt pattern. Select the size of the skirt pattern by your hip measurement. The following modifications create the slip pattern from the original skirt pattern:

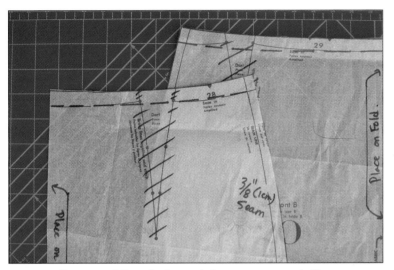

Cross out the darts and draw a new waistline

1. Cross out the darts of the pattern on the front and back, as they will not be sewn. This allows extra fabric for pulling on the slip over your hips. Draw a new, smooth waistline curve on the pattern.

2. Decide on the length of slip, and add 1-1/2" (3.8cm) for a hem allowance. The slip length may be determined by making it approximately 1" (2.5cm) shorter than the skirt with which it is to be worn.

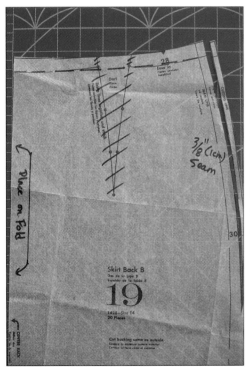

Mark the center back line as a fold and reduce the width of the seam allowance on both the front and back patterns.

3. The commercial pattern side seams are most likely 5/8" (1.5cm). For a slip, the best seam is 1/4" to 3/8" (0.6cm to 1cm). Reduce the pattern accordingly. The front and back each will be cut on the fold of the fabric. For a commercial skirt pattern with a center back zipper, the seamline becomes the fold line.

4. Now you are ready for the layout of the pattern on fabric and the sewing steps, starting on page 67.

You need to take the following body measurements to draft the slip pattern:

- ❖ waist circumference
- ❖ hip circumference
- ❖ waist to hip length
- ❖ slip length

1. Line 0-1 is the waist to hip length.

2. Line 0-2 is the slip length, from waist to hem.

3. Square a line from 0 to 3. This line equals (1/4 x hip) + 1" (2.5cm). Label this as the waistline.

4. Square a line from 1 to 4. This line is same length as 0-3 from step three. Label 1-4 as the hipline.

5. Square a line from 2 to 5. This line is same length as 0-3 from step three. Label 2-5 as the hemline.

6. Join point 3 to point 5 with a straight line.

7. Measure from point 0 to find point 6. This equals (1/4 x waist) +1" (2.5cm).

8. Line 6-7 is 1/2" (1.3cm).

9. Join point 0 to point 7 to create a waistline. The line needs to have a slight curve, ending at approximately the middle of line 0-6.

10. Join point 7 to point 4 with a curved line. This line becomes the side seam above the hip.

11. Optional design idea: an A-line slip is easily designed from the basic slip draft:

- ❖ Extend the hemline (line 2-5) by 1" to 1-1/2" (2.5cm to 3.8cm) past 5 to 8.
- ❖ Join point 8 to point 4 with a straight line. This is the side seam of the A-line slip. Be sure the overall line from 8 to 4 to 7 has a smooth, continuous shape, with no bends.

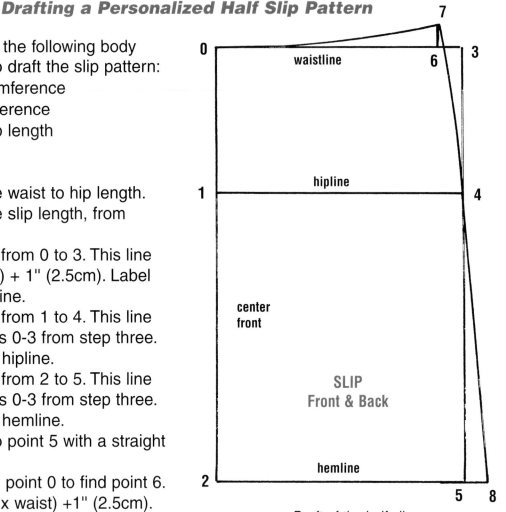

Draft of the half slip.

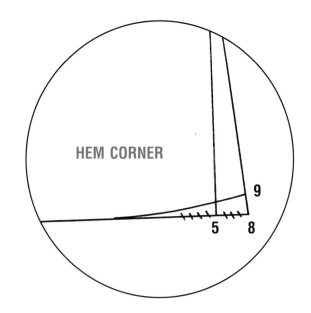

Corner detail on the half slip.

❖ The hemline must be shaped to ensure an attractive appearance and easy construction. Measure the length of line 4-5, and then measure this same length from 4 down toward 8 and mark as point 9 with a cross mark. Draw a long, gentle curve from 9 to line 2-5. This method allows the creation of a square corner at 9, thus making the hem shape at the side seam correct.

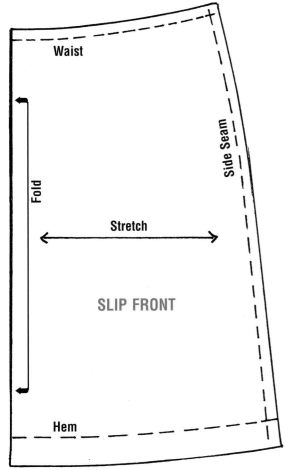

Add the seams and hems.

12. Complete the half slip pattern: The draft is complete. To make a pattern for layout and cutting, trace the slip draft onto tissue. You may wish to trace separate front and back patterns. Add 1/4" (.6cm) to the side seams and the waist edge. Add 1-1/2" (3.8cm) for a turned hem allowance. If you are going to use a lace finish at the hem edge, the hem allowance is not needed. (Note: These allowances are flexible; add different allowances, if you prefer.)

Fabric Required

To create the slip, you need to have the length of the slip plus 3" (7.5cm) of 60" (150cm) width fabric.

Layout

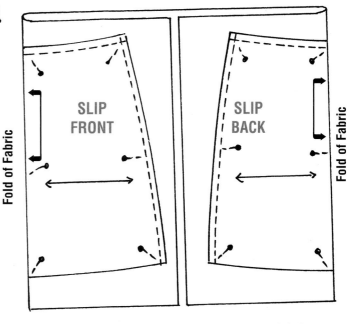

Layout of the slip, front and back, onto fabric.

Detailed Sewing Order of the Half Slip

1. Place the front and back right sides together, and sew one side seam using one of the seam stitching suggestions in Chapter 3 to create a smooth, flat seam.

2. If you wish to apply lace to the hem, it is best to do it now, when one side seam is still open. (Note: If you want a turned hem with no lace, wait until step 6.) There are two methods for adding lace to the slip's hem edge. Either the entire width of the lace is placed onto the tricot, or the lace is to hang down below the edge of the slip. For the second choice, in order to maintain the original length of the slip, cut off the width of the lace minus 1/2" (1.3cm). Lay the slip on a flat surface. Place the lace in the desired location on the hem. The secret for making the smoothest lace hem is in the pinning. As you pin,

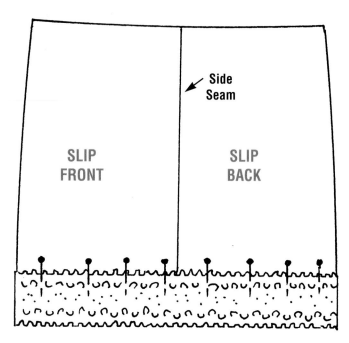

Pin the lace to the hem after one side seam has been sewn.

allow the lace to be slightly bigger than the tricot. For example, if you have 10" (25cm) of hem, you might have 10-1/8" (25.4cm) lace.

Sew the lace and the tricot together with a medium width plain zigzag or a multiple zigzag. Sew along the top and bottom if the lace is entirely on the tricot, and only along the top if the lace hangs down below the slip.

The "extra" lace trick works because, when lace is sewn to tricot, the open structure of the lace naturally tightens up slightly. If the lace is the same size as the tricot, it will pucker slightly when sewn, and pull in the tricot.

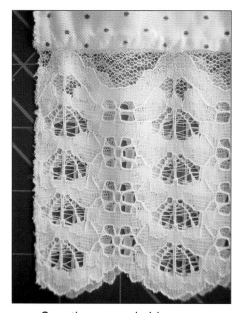

Sew the second side seam.

Press the seam to the back of the slip and topstitch.

3. Sew the second side seam. This joins the ends of the lace together in the seam. Lightly press the seams to the back. Topstitch the seam allowance in the lace hem area to the back of the slip—this creates a durable seam.

4. This is an excellent time for a fitting. Look under Fitting Solutions, page 71.

5. Finish the waist edge with elastic. Cut the elastic 1-1/2" to 4" (3.8cm to 10.2cm) smaller than your waist. Test the length for comfort. Sew the ends of the elastic together (see page 25, Chapter 3, for a hint about sewing elastic).

Mark the slip and elastic into quarters or eighths, and use one of the following techniques for applying the elastic:

Mark the elastic and slip waist edge into quarters or eighths.

❖ For completely hidden elastic, lay the elastic onto the wrong side of the top edge of the slip. Match the quarter pin marks. Sew on the lower edge of the elastic. Fold the elastic and fabric to the inside of the slip and sew on the lower edge again.

❖ This second method is to be used when you want the elastic to show. This is great when you have found a colored tricot and elastic or stretch lace in a matching color. Lay the elastic onto the right side of the slip. No fabric should extend past the top of the elastic. Match the quarter pin marks.

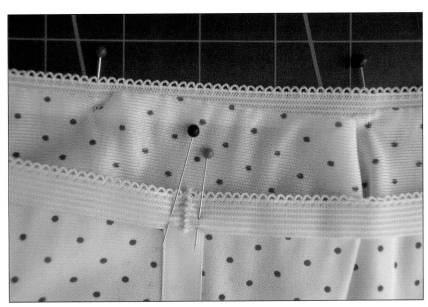

Place a ribbon between the elastic and the slip.

❖ To hide the join in the elastic, place a short piece of 1/2" (1.3cm) wide satin ribbon between the elastic and the slip.

Sew along the elastic's lower edge. Wrap satin ribbon around the elastic to the inside of the slip and tack by sewing a square or an X. The join in elastics often pulls apart in wearing—this method helps to solve the problem.

❖ For picot edge elastic and enclosed waistline raw edges, use this method. With elastic sewn into a circle and quartered with pins, place it to the wrong side of the slip, matching the lower edge of elastic to the slip's upper edge. Stitch the elastic in place along the picot edge with a medium width stitch. Carefully trim the seam allowances off the slip and turn the elastic to the right side. Stitch the free edge into place in the fabric. The picot edge sits attractively along the top edge of the slip.

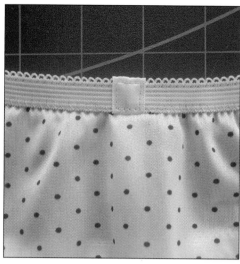

Tack the ribbon by sewing a square or an X.

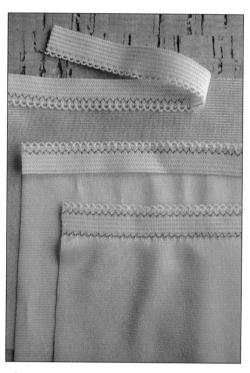

Method for picot edge elastic.

Hem ideas for slips.

6. If you prefer, you may use a traditional turned hem on the slip. The turned hem finish is excellent because it adds weight, and makes a durable finish. The 1-1/2" (3.8cm) hem of the slip is pressed to the wrong side and stitched. Use a twin needle from the right side to make a very attractive, stretchy, professional look. The multiple zigzag works well, or test the various stitches your machine has to create a decorative effect. Keep in mind the fabric is light-weight, and often "less is best."

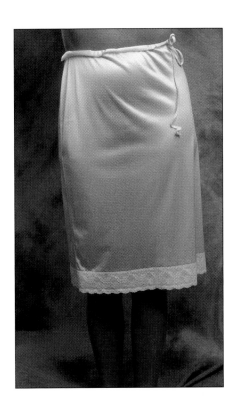

The slip hangs crookedly.

Problem #1: The slip hangs crookedly. The most important feature of the slip is to have the hem of the slip parallel with the floor. A fuller tummy, high hip, and a large seat are some of the body's special variations that could cause the slip to hang crookedly. Plus-sized figures often have a lower waistline position in the front as compared to the back. This makes the hem droop down in the front and lift up in the back. The side seam also swings toward the back, creating an unattractive appearance.

A figure with one high hip will have the slip shorter on one side than the other.

Solution: For all of these challenges, try on the slip and stand in front of a full-length mirror! Tie a piece of narrow elastic around your waist and over the slip. Your main goal is to adjust the level of the slip at the waist to make the hem parallel to the floor. You will notice that as you correct the hem, the side seams will hang straight down the sides of the body. Examine the fit from the front, sides and back.

The important lesson to learn is that the adjustment is made at the waist. When you know the correct location of the waist, mark the new waist on the slip and transfer the new markings to your pattern. Be careful to label your pattern with front, back, left and right for easy use in the future. (Note: This tip is valuable for a fitted skirt as well.)

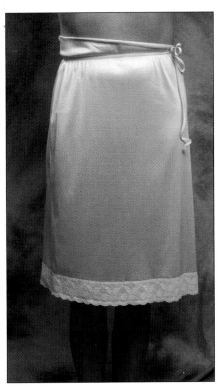

The waist is corrected to improve the fit.

Problem #2: The elastic around your waist needs to be tighter or looser.

Solution: The amount of elastic used may need to be changed. Also remember that you could use elastic stretch lace. It has a softer, non-binding feel, and may be used instead of elastic.

Problem #3: When you are walking, the slip creeps up your body. This happens because there is not enough ease through the hip area, or the figure may have a larger measurement around the thighs than hips.

Solution: Add extra ease to the side seams of the slip pattern, or if the thigh area is full, the slip may fit more comfortably with a slight A-line shape. A turned-up hem (without lace) may also help prevent the slip's creeping up the legs.

Elastic stretch lace on the waist edge of a slip.

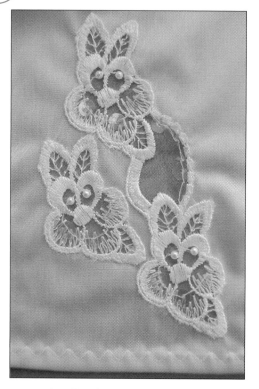

Appliqué lace onto the fabric.

Variations

1. Add appliqué detail above the hem area of the slip. Sew around appliqués with a narrow, plain zigzag or the multiple zigzag. You can cut apart lace trim to create appliqué sections. The fabric of the slip may be cut out from behind the appliqué to make a sheer section.

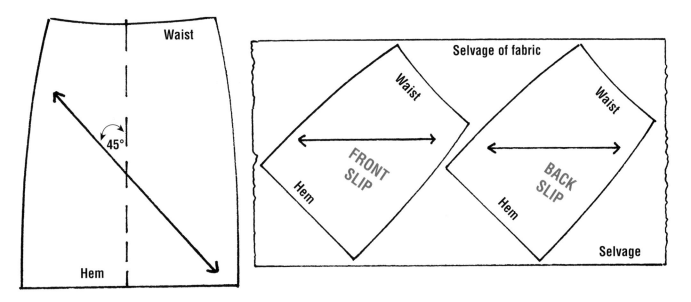

2. Use the half slip pattern and cut it on the bias direction of a woven fabric. For the easiest layout, trace the draft of your slip pattern in full width so you don't have to fold the fabric in half. Draw a grain line on the traced paper pattern. Draw it at a 45° angle to the center line of the slip pattern. This is your guide for accurate cutting.

The slip is comfortable because the bias cutting direction has ease and give. Since woven fabric is used for this variation, you will be able to select from many more fabrics. A light, cotton slip helps the body stay cool in hot climates. Silk has a feel all its own.

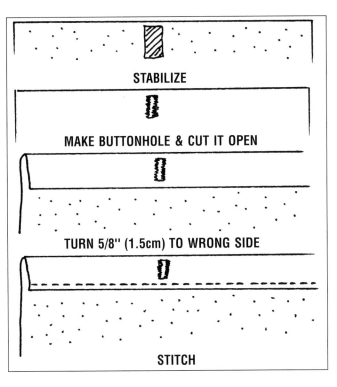

Make a casing.

3. Create a casing at the waist of the slip. This is an excellent method for people who fluctuate in weight, or for a gift, when the exact waist size is not known.

Make a 3/8" (1cm) machine buttonhole at the center back of the slip's waist edge. To prevent the buttonhole from stretching, press a small rectangle of interfacing in place first. Cut the buttonhole open.

Turn down and lightly press 5/8" (1.5cm) of fabric at the slip's waist edge to the inside, and then stitch it into place. Use a regular straight stitch or a slight zigzag, or sew from the right side with a twin needle.

The elastic may now be run through the casing using the buttonhole opening, and you will always have easy access to the elastic if its size needs to be changed.

Layout of pattern onto woven fabric.

Six-Panel Slip with Godets

An elegant and feminine design, the six-panel slip is beautiful. The slip is constructed of six pieces of the panel pattern and six pieces of the godet pattern. Nylon tricot or any other soft knit that hangs well are good fabric choices for the panel. The godet is an inset piece, sewn between the panels. It can be made in lace, chiffon, or any soft fabric. The godets could also be made in the same fabric as the slip. The hem is finished by using a narrow lace trim. This is a very easy pattern to draft.

Six-panel slip.

Draft the Six-Panel Slip with Godets

You will need to take the following body measurements to draft the pattern:

- ❖ waist circumference
- ❖ hip circumference
- ❖ waist to hip length
- ❖ slip length

Draft the Panel

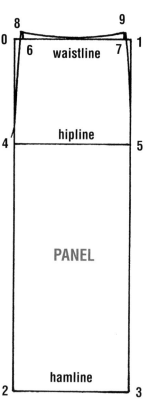

1. Draw a line from 0 to 1. The length is (hip plus 4") divided by 6. Label this as the waistline.

2. Square a line from 0 to 2 and from 1 to 3. These lines are the desired slip length.

3. Join point 2 to point 3. Label this line as the hemline.

4. Measure from point 0 to find point 4 and from point 1 to point 5. Both of these lengths are equal to the waist to hip measurement.

Join 4 to 5 with a line. Label this line as the hip line.

5. Calculate the shaping needed for the waist:

a). Waist measurement of the figure plus 4" (10cm) = X

b). X divided by 6 (because there are 6 panels in the slip) = size of each panel at the waist

6. Along line 0 to 1, mark 6 and 7. The distance between 6 and 7 is the length found above, in 5b). Center the amount so that it shapes each side of the rectangle by the same amount.

7. Draw lines from 6 up to 8 and from 7 up to 9. These lines are 1/4" (6cm).

8. Join 8 to 4 and 9 to 5 with curved lines.

9. Join 8 to 9 with a curved line. The middle of the curve must touch line 0-1.

10. Complete the pattern by adding 1/4" to the long sides of the panel.

Draft the Godet

1. Line 1-2 is 9" to 12" (23cm to 30cm), the desired length of the godet.

2. Square a line from 2 to 3 that is 3" to 4" (8cm to 10cm).

3. Square a line from 2 to 4 that is 3" to 4" (8cm to 10cm).

4. Join 1 to 3 and 1 to 4 with straight lines.

5. To have a good hem shape on the godet, measure from 1 to find 5 and from 1 to find 6. These distances from 1 to 5 and 1 to 6 must equal the length of line 1-2. Draw a curve from 5 to 6 and have the curve touch point 2.

6. Complete the pattern by adding a 1/4" (.6cm) seam to the edges numbered 1-5 and 1-6. No hem allowance is needed.

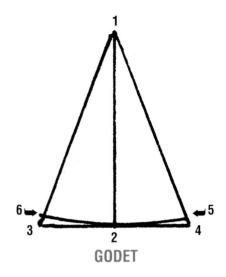

GODET

Tip: For an easier time of sewing the godets to the panels, add an extra 1/4" (.6cm) seam where the panel and the godet will join. For accuracy, measure the godet pattern from point 1 to 5. This gives you the length of the extra 1/4" (.6cm) seam allowance needed on the panel.

Fabric Required

To sew this slip, you need fabric equivalent to the length of the slip plus 3" (7.5cm), for 60"(150cm) width fabric, for the panels and about 1/4 yard (.25M) for the godets.

Lay out the pattern, and cut six panels and six godets.

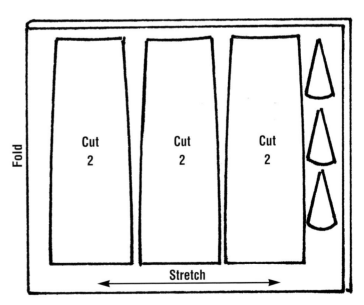

Layout of the six-panel slip.

Detailed Sewing Order for the Six-Panel Slip

1. Pin one godet to the left side of one panel, with the right sides together. Stitch from the hem toward the top of the godet. Use 1/4" (0.6cm) seam. Press the seams open, and press the seam allowance toward the panel.

2. Pin and sew the other five panels and godets following the procedure from the first.

3. Sew the six seams that join the six panels. Sew from the hem toward the waist edge.

4. Finish the hem edge. Lap narrow lace onto the right side of the fabric and stitch it into place. The hemline curves, so select 3/8" to 3/4" (1cm to 2cm) wide lace. These are best for pinning and shaping around curves.

5. Sew the elastic to the waist edge of the slip. Refer to step 5 in the detailed sewing order for the half slip (page 69) for more details.

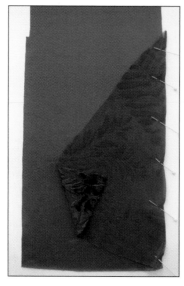

Pin godet to panel.

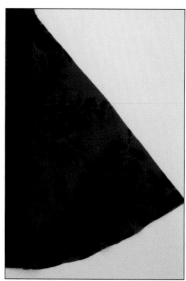

Stitch and press.

Sew the panels together.

The sewn panels and godet.

Lap lace onto hem edge, pin and stitch.

Chapter 7

Bra Top

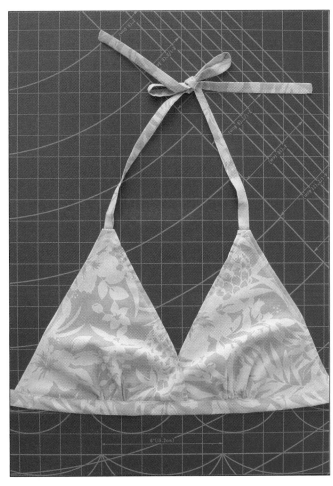

Designed for simple sewing and an attractive fit, the bra top is suitable for many fabrics. Make a bra top to match a pair of boxers for a sleep set, or create a panties and bra set. Woven cotton, polyester, knit cottons, stretch laces and nylon tricot are all good fabric choices. The basic bra top needs only fabric and thread. No special notions are required, although there are many options for variations in straps, hooks, trims and elastics.

The great challenge in fitting V-necklines is to prevent their stretching, and so the bra top has been designed with the straight of grain of a woven fabric or the lengthwise direction of a knit along the V-neck to help the fabric lie smoothly over the body. The bra design may be either a single or double fabric layer. It has gathers under the bust and straps that could tie at the back of the neck or attach to a band around the body. The pattern may not be suitable for heavy breasted figures, because it may not provide the support desired.

The grid drawing of the bra top pattern is included here in half-scale. Seam allowances are included in the pattern. There are two ways to make the full scale pattern you will use for sewing:

1. Use a photocopier: Set the copier to x200. Place this book into the machine and make a copy. The patterns will fit onto 11" x 17" paper. The pattern has grain-lines and foldlines and is ready for layout and cutting.

2. Draw the pattern onto 1" (2.5cm) grid paper. One square on the grid equals 1" (2.5cm). Count out the squares to draw the basic shape of the pattern first, and then draw curves and shapes using a curved ruler along with the grid as your guide.

Size 1		Size 2		
32	A	B	C	D
34	A	B	C	D
36	A	B	C	D
38	A	B	C	D
40	A	B	C	
			Size 3	

This chart gives a suggestion for the size of bra top to select. Personal fit is an important part of bra fitting. The breast shape, body length and the amount you want to be covered (or uncovered!) all need to be measured and test fitted.

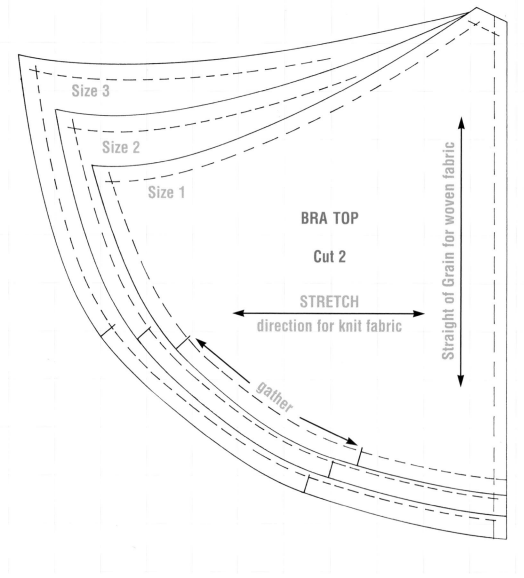

Bra top.

Fabric Required:
2/3 yard (0.6M) of 45" width

Layout and Cutting for the Single Layer Bra Top

1-1/2" X 20" (3.8cm X 50.7cm)

2-1/4" X 20" (6cm X 50.7cm)

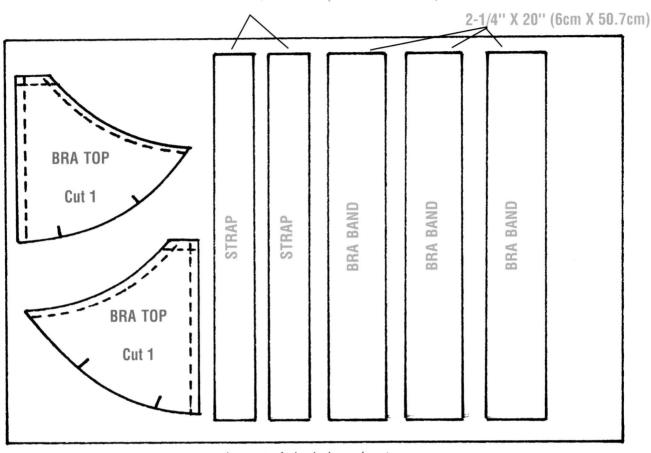

Layout of single layer bra top.

Cut the following:
- ❖ Three bra bands 2-1/4" (6cm) wide and 20" (50.7cm) long.
- ❖ Two straps 1-1/2" (3.8cm) wide and 20" (50.7cm) long. (Hint: These bands and straps are cut on the fabric's lengthwise grain for the best pressing, sewing and wearing results.)
- ❖ Two bra tops.

Detailed Sewing Order for Bra Top with Single Fabric Layer

1. For knits, sew 3/8" (1cm) elastic to the wrong side of the two top edges of the bra top. Turn and topstitch.

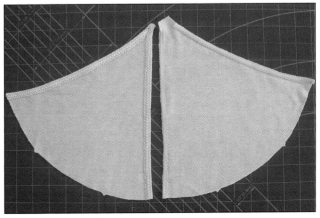

For knit fabrics, sew elastic to the edges.

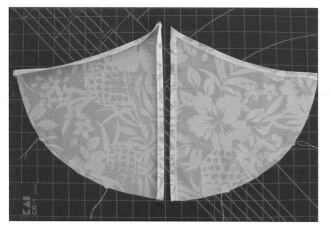

For woven fabrics, serge to finish.

For woven fabrics, finish the two angled edges with a zigzag stitch or by serging. Turn 3/8" (1cm) to the wrong side and topstitch. A twin needle is particularly useful for this step, as it makes an attractive finish.

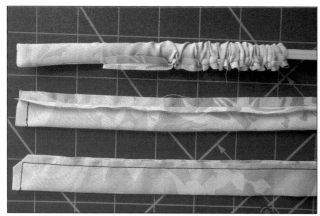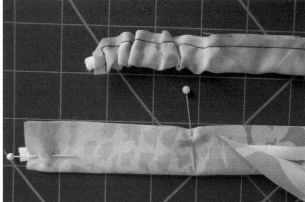

Make straps.

2. Construct straps by folding the fabric, right sides together. Sew a 1/4" (.6cm) seam along the long edge and across one end. Because one end of the strap is finished when it is sewn closed, you can turn the tube with the blunt end of a knitting needle or a chopstick—or, lay 1/4" twill tape in the strap and sew it to the end of the strap during the sewing step. Pull the twill tape to turn the strap, and simply cut off the tape from the right side. Press the straps flat.

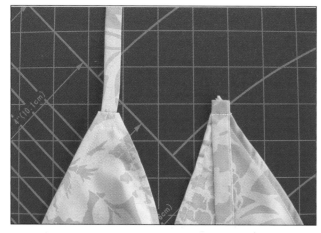

Sew straps to the bra.

3. Pin and sew the unfinished ends of the straps to the short, straight edge of the top of the bra. Pull the strap up into the wearing position, and topstitch across the edge of the bra top to hold the seams in place.

4. Sew a gathering stitching line between the notches.

5. Using the gathering thread, pull the fabric in until it measures:
   8-1/2" (21.6cm) for size 1
   10-1/2" (26.6cm) for size 2
   12" (30.5cm) for size 3

6. Overlap the two bra sections at the center by these measurements:
   1-1/4" (3.2cm) for size 1
   2" (5cm) for size 2
   2-3/4" (7cm) for size 3
   Machine baste the two layers together.

Gather the lower edge of the bra top and overlap at the center.

7. Sew three bra band sections together with 1/4" (.6cm) seams, and press the seams open. The bra band will be easiest to sew if it is prepared accurately by pressing.
   a) Press the band in half lengthwise.
   b) Open out the band and draw a seam line 3/4" (2cm) from the fold.
   c) Lay the band on your ironing board and fold the band in half again, on the original fold from step a). Then, fold and press under the seam allowance on the side of the band that has no line drawn. You don't have to measure, just line up the fold with the drawn line. Press carefully.

Fold and press the bra band.

8. Unfold the bra band. Pin the right side of the edge that has drawn line to the right side of the bra top.

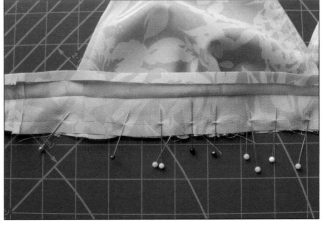

Pin the bra band to the bra top.

*Sew the bra band to the
bra top.*

*Press the band away from
the top.*

*Fold the band to the inside of the
bra top and topstitch.*

9. Sew the layers along the drawn line. It is a 3/8" (1cm) seam. Make the straps and finish bra band.

a) Press the bra band away from the bra.

b) Wrap the bra band to the wrong side of the bra sections, pin.

c) Fold the seam lines of straps in and pin to the end of each strap.

d) Topstitch the band and the straps close to the two folded edges. A straight stitch, narrow zigzag, decorative machine stitch, and embroi-dery stitches are all possibilities for finishing.

Layout and Cutting for the Double Layer Bra Top

1-1/2" X 20" (3.8cm X 50.7cm)

2-1/4" X 20" (6cm X 50.7cm)

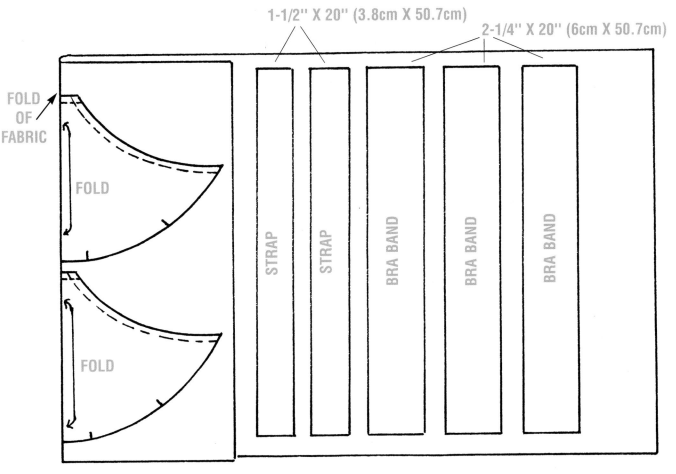

Layout for the double layer bra top.

Cut the following:

❖ Three bra bands 2-1/4" (6cm) wide and 20" (50.7cm) long.

❖ Two straps 1-1/2" (3.8cm) wide and 20" (50.7cm) long. (Hint: Cut these bands and straps on the fabric's lengthwise grain for the best pressing, sewing and wearing results.)

❖ Two bra tops. On the pattern, remove the seam allowance along the neckline edge and place the pattern on the fold of the fabric for cutting.

Detailed Sewing of the Double Layer Bra Top

1. Stay stitch 3/8" (1cm) from the edge to reinforce the small V shape at the top of bra. Clip into the point of the V.

2. Make the straps (see step 2, page 80).

Stay stitch.

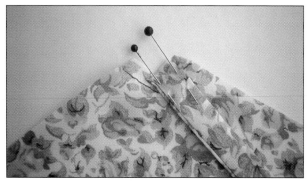

Pin the straps to the right side of the bra.

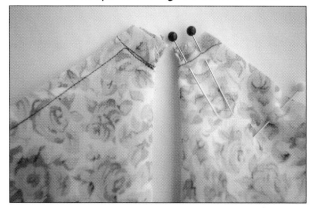

Fold the bra top in half and stitch.

Trim, turn the bra top right side out.

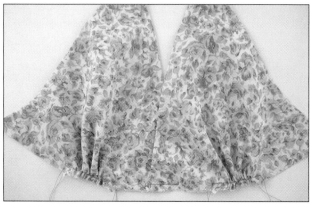

Gather the lower edges and overlap.

3. Pin the straps to the right side of the bra sections. Line up the unfinished square end of the strap to the short straight edge. The clip into the V allows the strap to sit at the fold edge of bra.

4. Fold the bra, right sides together, with the straps lying in-between. Sew the side area from the lower edge up, toward the top of the bra. Turn the corner and sew across the short, straight line to secure the strap and the two layers of the bra top.

> ***Tip:*** to prevent stretching, cut a 1/4" (0.6cm) wide by 8" (20.3cm) long piece of self fabric, and sew over it when stitching along the side area of bra.

5. Trim the seams, turn the bra right side out and press.

6. Understitch the bra seam. Understitching is a line of straight sewing, 1/8"(0.3cm) from the seam line, catching only facing and seam allowances. The area near the strap is very hard to reach when understitching—just sew as far as possible.

7. Turn the bra right side out and press.

8. Through two layers of fabric and between the notches, sew a gathering line, a scant 3/8" (1cm) from the raw edges.

9. Using the gathering threads, pull the fabric in until it measures:

8-1/2" (21.6cm) for size 1
10-/2" (26.6cm) for size 2
12" (30.5cm) for size 3

10. Overlap the two bra sections at the center by these measurements:

1-1/4" (3.2cm) for size 1
2"-(5cm) for size 2
2-3/4" (7cm) for size 3

Machine baste the two layers together.

11. Sew three bra band sections together and prepare the band as described in the previous section, in steps 7, 8 and 9, on pages 81-82.

12. The bra may be worn with the straps tied around the neck, or the straps may go over the shoulders. Fit the bra top, and position the correct strap length. Sew a loop in the end of each shoulder strap, and thread the around-the-body-band through it.

Fitting Solutions

This is an easy design to test for fit, because the pattern piece is so simple. Here are the details you may wish to check:

Problem #1: The amount of fabric in your bra top is not quite perfect—you do not feel it covers enough, or it covers too much.

Solution: Change the size you have selected—or, you could fold under the extra fabric in the test copy to create a smaller bra top, or cut a new bra, adding more fabric in the places you feel it should be added.

Problem #2: The gathers do not lie under the fullest part of the bust.

Solution: The gathers are the fitting features that give shape to the bra top. If they are too far toward the side of the body, you may need to overlap the two bra tops more at the center front. If the gathers appear too close to the center front, the bra tops can be overlapped by less.

If you like the overlap and the neckline you have created, you might move the gathers so they create a good fit for your body. After finding the best combination of gathers and overlap, mark the solutions on your pattern for future sewing. Also note on the pattern whether the fabric used was knit or woven, as this certainly affects the fit of the bra.

Variations

1. The straps may be plush back elastic or decorative elastics in various colors. Safety pin the straps to the bra band to check for a comfortable length. Attach straps as shown in this photo.

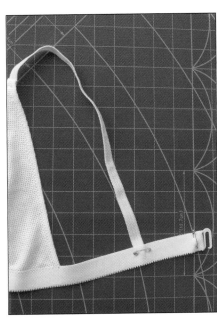

Use elastic for the bra band.

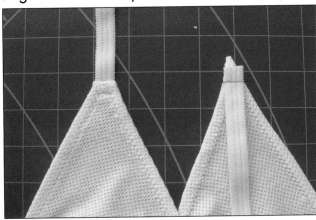

Use elastic for the straps.

Serge the lower edge and then add elastic.

2. Change the bra band to elastic stretch lace or plush back elastic. For this variation, an optional step would be to serge the gathered edge after it has been gathered to the lengths suggested in the sewing steps. This produces the least bulky finish. The elastic stretch lace is then lapped onto the bra's lower edge, and the layers are sewn together with a medium width zigzag. Use a thread color to match the elastic or lace for an invisible effect.

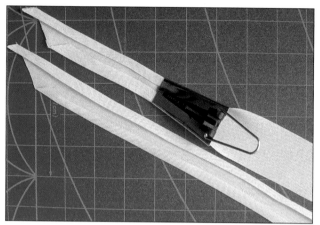

Make bias tape.

3. Cut off the seams allowed at the side of the bra, and finish the edges with double-fold bias binding. Purchased binding is fine, or make your own self fabric binding by pressing the trim as it runs through a bias tape maker.

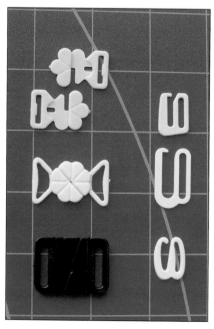

Various types of hooks.

4. The bra band ends that surround the body are usually made of self fabric. You might thread an elastic through the self fabric. The self fabric could then be shirred up slightly and sewn. This is then a stretchy band around the body. The trick to this is to sew the straps closed, then thread the elastic and then sew the bra band below the bra top last. A bra hook or swim hook is a great way for this type of band to close.

Chapter 8

Panties

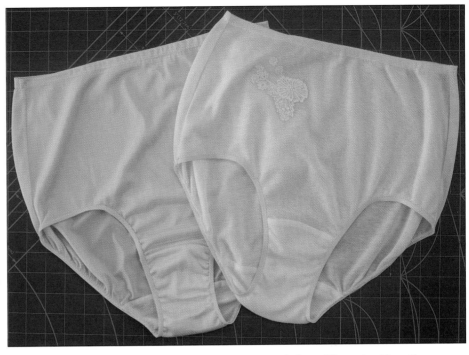

Panties are one of our most important lingerie items, and for this reason, we expect a lot of them. We expect good panties to fit well, to be attractive and comfortable, and they also have to be durable and easy to care for. This chapter is dedicated to measuring the body, drafting a Classic Ladies' Panties Pattern for your measurements, explaining the features of fit, showing all the construction details and showing possible design variations. Five sizes of the Classic Panties pattern are also included in a half scale grid pattern at the end of the chapter.

Features of Classic Panties

The drafting methods and the pattern have been devised for use with cotton knits and nylon tricot—fabrics that offer a degree of crosswise stretch. The panties are designed to sit at the waist of the figure and around the normal leg line. It is an excellent basic style for working out and solving any personal fitting challenges you might have.

Many women select these panties as their favorite design for everyday wear. Many others prefer variations of these panties that are briefer, and/or have higher cut legs. These alterations are all possible. I encourage you to use these Classic Panties as your favorite basic pattern or use it as you might any basic block, from which other styles may be developed.

Measuring the Body

Four measurements are needed to draft the Classic Ladies' Panties pattern. Take all of the necessary measurements comfortably, wearing panties, a slip or another smooth-fitting garment. Stand in front of a mirror—in fact, it may even be better to have a friend do the measuring for you. Write each of the four measurements down, along with the date and your weight.

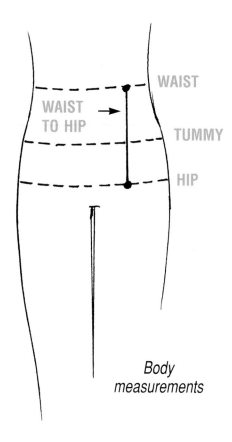

Body measurements

1. **The waist:** Measure the place around your body where it tapers in.

2. **The hip:** Measure around the fullest part of the seat—the tape measure will often go over the hip joint on the side of the body.

The hip will be about 6" to 9" (15.4cm to 23cm) below the level of the waist. This great amount of variation results from different body heights and proportions.

Note: If the figure has a more dominant tummy than seat, the fullest part of the body may be higher than the hip level described above.

If this is the case, measure the full tummy, and that measurement will be used in drafting.

3. **The waist to hip:** Measure the length on the body between the waistline you measured and the hipline you measured. Even if you used a tummy measurement as the fullest part of the body, you still need the length from hip to waist.

4. **The crotch depth:** this measurement is taken while you are seated on a flat surface. Measure from the flat surface, up the side seam position of your body to the waist.

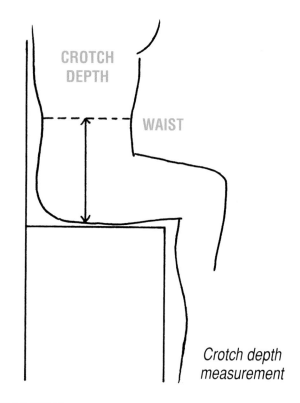

Crotch depth measurement

The charts that follow give you a representative sample of the measurements you might obtain in the regular and plus size range.

As with all measurements, we rarely fit into one exact category. They do, however, give you a guide and a point of comparison. They would also allow you to draft a standard size (if there is such a thing). The first chart is in English measurements (inches), and the second is in metric (centimeters).

English measurements for a 5' 6" figure

Waist	22''	24''	26''	28''	30''	32''	34''	36''	38''	40''
Hip	32''	34''	36''	38''	40''	42''	44''	46''	48''	50''
Waist-to-hip	7-3/4''	7-3/4''	8''	8''	8-1/4''	8-1/4''	8-1/2''	8-1/2''	8-3/4''	8-3/4''
Crotch depth	10-1/2''	10-1/2''	11''	11''	11-1/2''	11-1/2''	12''	12''	12-1/2''	12-1/2''

Metric measurements for a 168cm figure

Waist	56cm	61cm	66cm	71cm	76cm	81cm	86.5cm	91.5cm	96.5cm	101cm
Hip	81cm	86.5cm	91.5cm	96.5cm	101.5cm	106.5cm	112cm	117cm	122cm	127cm
Waist-to-hip	19.5cm	19.5cm	20.4cm	20.4cm	21cm	21cm	21.6cm	21.6cm	22.2cm	22.2cm
Crotch depth	26.7cm	26.7cm	28cm	28cm	29.3cm	29.3cm	30.6cm	30.6cm	31.8cm	31.8cm

Drafting Classic Ladies' Panties

1. Line 0-1 equals (hip divided by 2) - 3/4" (2cm) ease. Label this as the waistline.

2. Line 0-2 is (1/2 x measurement of line 0-1) + 3/4" (2cm).

3. Square a line from 2 to 3. This line is waist to hip - 3/4" (2cm). Label this line as the side seam.

4. Square a line from 1 to 4. This line is the crotch depth + 3" (7.5cm). Label this line as the center front fold.

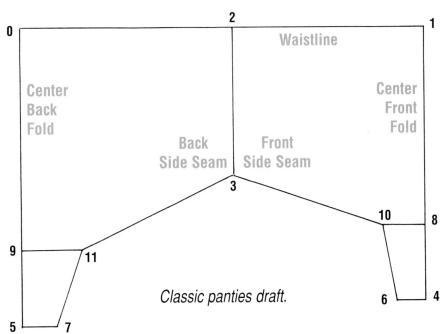

Classic panties draft.

5. Square a line from 0 to 5. This line is the crotch depth + 4-3/4" (12cm). Label this as the center back fold.

Note: 2-3, 1-4 and 0-5 will all be parallel to one another.

6. Square a line from lines 4-6 and 5-7. Select a measurement from this chart for the length of the line:

   1-1/2" for 32"-38" hip (3.8cm for 81cm-96.5cm hip)
   1-5/8" for 40"-44" hip (4.2cm for 101.5cm to 112cm hip)
   1-3/4" for 46"-50" hip (4.5cm for 117cm to 127cm hip)

7. Measure from point 4 to find point 8. The distance is 4" (10cm). Measure from 5 to find point 9. The distance is 4" (10cm).

8. Square a line from line 8-10. Select a measurement from this chart for the length of the line:

   2" for 32"-38" hip (3.8cm for 81cm-96.5cm hip)
   2-1/4" for 40"-44" hip (5.8cm for 101.5cm-112cm hip)
   2-1/2" for 46"-50" hip (6.5cm for 117cm-127cm hip)

   Square a line from line 9-11. Select a measurement from this chart for the length of the line:

   3-1/2" for 32"-38" hip (9cm for 81cm-96.5cm hip)
   3-3/4" for 40"-44" hip (9.6cm for 101.5cm-112cm hip)
   4" for 46"-50" hip (10.2cm for 117cm-127cm hip)

9. Draw guidelines from 6 to 10 to 3 to 11 to 7.

10. Calculate the waist shape, and then you will use amount "Z" in step 11:

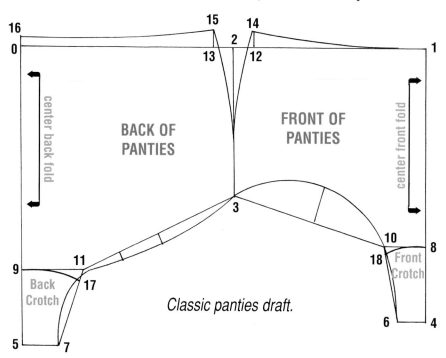

Classic panties draft.

a). hip minus waist = X (for example, hip 38" minus waist 28" = 10" or, 96.5cm hip minus 71cm waist = 25.5cm)

b). X minus 4" (10cm) ease = Y (10"-4" = 6", or 25.6cm - 10.2cm = 15.4cm)

c). Y divided by 4 = Z (6" divided by 4 = 1-1/2", or 15.4cm divided by 4 = 3.8cm)

d). Z is the amount of shaping for the front and back waist (1-1/2", or 3.8cm)

11. Measure from point 2 to find point 12. Measure from point 2 to find point 13. The distance for each of these measurements is Z (from step 10).

12. Square a line from line 12-14 and from line 13-15. These lines are both 1/2" (1.3cm) to 3/4" (2cm).

13. Square a line from line 0-16. This line is 1/4" (.6cm) to 3/8" (1cm).

14. Draw a gentle curve for the front waist from point 14 to point 1.
Draw another curve for the back waist from point 15 to point 16.

15. Draw the front and back side seams by joining point 14 to line 2-3, and then point 15 to line 2-3. The upper sections of the side seams are curved, so that they blend smoothly into line 2-3.

16. Using the guidelines drawn in step 8, draft the curve of the leg. Keep in mind that the overall curve must be smooth to give an attractive and comfortable leg design, so the measurements in the following steps (a to d) are flexible.

a). From 6 to 10, curve the front leg line inward by approximately 1/8" (0.3cm).

b). Find the middle of line 10-3, and square a line upward 2" (5cm) to 2-1/2" (6.5cm). Draw the panties' curve.

c). Measure and mark the line from point 3 to point 11 into quarters. Square a 5/8" to 3/4" (1.5 to 2cm) line down from the middle mark. From the quarter mark closest to point 11, square a 3/8" (1cm) line down. Draw the curve of the panties' leg.

d). From point 11 to point 7, curve the back leg line inward by 1/4" (0.6cm).

17. Draw the back crotch seam line curve, from point 9 to point 17. Point 17 is below point 11 by 3/8" (1cm). Draw the front crotch seam line curve from point 8 to point 18. Point 18 is below point 10 by 3/8" (1cm).

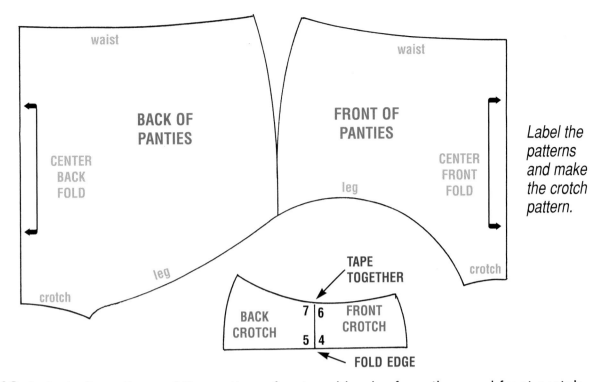

Label the patterns and make the crotch pattern.

18. Label all sections of the pattern: front and back of panties, and front crotch and back crotch.

19. Cut the draft apart along the crotch seam lines, line 8-18 and line 9-17. Tape the two pieces together along lines 4-6 and 5-7. Label the long, straight line as the fold edge.

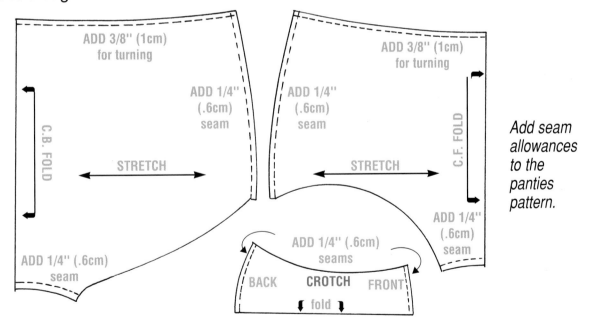

Add seam allowances to the panties pattern.

20. The draft is complete—now it needs seam allowances. Trace the front, back and crotch onto tissue and add 1/4" (0.6cm) allowance to the side seams and all crotch seams. Add 3/8" (1cm) to the waist edges of the front and back of the panties. The leg edges on the panties and crotch do not require an added allowance, because the elastic is lapped, and no turning is required.

Fabric Required

Patterns for panties vary in style and length of pattern pieces, and widths of available fabrics vary greatly. Yardage charts are not an exact science! The great feature of panties is the efficiency with which you can lay out the pattern and cut the fabric. After sewing and testing the first pair, you will have determined the amount of fabric you need to construct your preferred style and design. To begin, try 1/2 yard (0.5M) of 60" (150cm) width fabric.

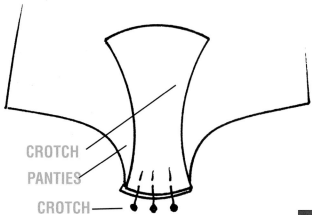

Detailed Sewing Order of Classic Panties

1. Front crotch seam: Place the right side of the crotch to the right side of panties' front. Place the right side of the lining crotch to the wrong side of the panties' front. Pin all the layers carefully and accurately together, and stitch by serging or sewing with a very narrow zigzag.

Pull the crotch sections away from the panties and press lightly to smooth and flatten the seam.

2. Place, pin, sew and press the back crotch pieces onto the panties' back following the procedure described for the front. Note: When placing the lining crotch to the panties, wrap it around the sections of the panties, allowing the three crotch seam edges to be exposed. This makes it easier to sew.

The completed front crotch seam.

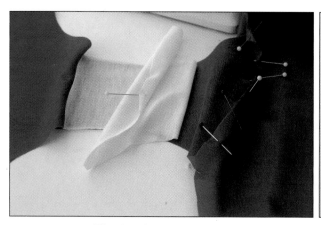

The back crotch seam.

The back crotch seam, pinned.

3. Sew the two layers of the crotch together along the leg edges, as close as you can to the raw edge, with a narrow zigzag. Trim away the lining crotch to even the edges. This makes for easier leg elastic application.

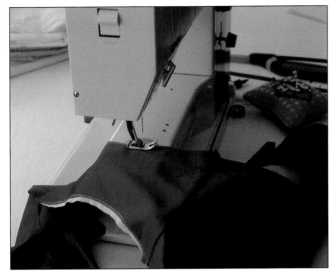

Sew the lining crotch along the leg edges.

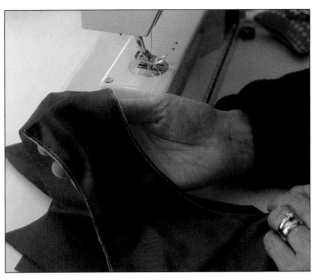

Trim away extra fabric.

4. Leg elastic: These panties are made with the elastic showing on the right side of the leg. This design detail is great when you have a colored fabric with matching elastic—and it also produces the thinnest leg finish, with no turning of the fabric. This makes for less bulk (greater comfort!) and less sewing.

Cut elastic 2-1/2" to 4" (6.5cm to 10.2cm) shorter than the circumference of your leg. Test the elastic around your leg for comfort.

Pin the elastic to the right side of the panties' edge using the following measurement suggestions. Stitch with a plain, medium-width zigzag.

• Across the front leg, you should have 1/4" to 1/2" (0.6cm to 1.3cm) less elastic than the edge of the panties.

• In the crotch area, you should use 3/4" to 1" (2cm to 2.5cm) less elastic than panties edge.

• Across the back of the leg, you should have 1-1/2" to 2-1/2" (3.8cm to 6.5cm) less elastic than panties edge.

Stretch the elastic to fit the fabric, and stitch (refer to chapter 3, page 25 for more information).

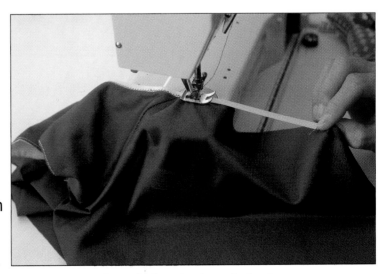

Stretch the elastic to fit the leg.

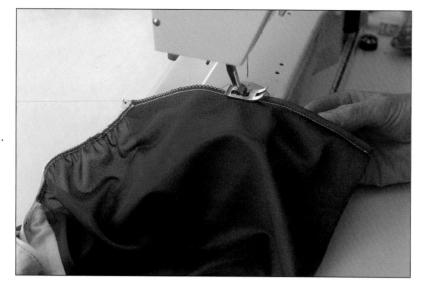

Sew one side seam.

5. Place the front and back of the panties' right sides together, and sew only one of the side seams.

Pin the elastic to the waist edge of the panties.

6. For the waistline of the panties, cut the elastic 1-1/2" to 4" (3.8cm to 10.2cm) smaller than your waist. Test the length for comfort. Mark the elastic and edge of the panties into quarters. Lay the elastic on the wrong side of the panties, match quarter markings, and pin them together.

Sew the elastic to the panties.

7. Sew the first row of stitching.

8. Place the front and back of the panties right sides together, and sew the second side seam (note—this is a good time to test fit your first pair).

9. Fold down the elastic at the waist, and stitch the second row. This method creates a durable side seam, and hides the ends of the elastic.

Fold the elastic and fabric to the wrong side of the panties and stitch again.

The completed leg edges.

10. Fold, pin and stitch the leg elastic seam allowance to the back of the panties. Stitch through all the layers to reinforce and keep the elastic flat.

Fitting Solutions

Testing the fit of your draft is an important step. Try the panties on your body after step 6 in the construction order. Here are four areas to evaluate, and the solutions for stumbling blocks you might encounter:

Problem #1: When you check the length of the panties, you discover that it does not sit well at your waist—there is not enough length at the center waist, or too much at the center back, etc.

Solution: Adjust the level of the waist elastic. Since only one row of stitching has been done, now is a good time to make adjustments. Move, walk and sit wearing the panties and decide whether the elastic is where you want it around the waist. If your need to make changes, move the elastic to a more comfortable place. Draw the new lines in red on your tissue pattern or on your draft. Many waistlines are not level with the floor. A round-tummied figure with a high waist needs extra length at the center front of the pattern, to raise the waistline. This line will usually be tapered down toward the side seams. Anywhere from 3/8" to 2" (1cm-5cm) could be added. Other figures have a low front waist and for them, the center front length of the panties needs to be shortened. These changes create a personalized, comfortable pattern.

Problem #2: When you check the width of the panties, you discover that the fabric does not sit well around the hip and waist area. It does not fit comfortably, or it feels too tight or too loose.

Solution: Redraw the side seam of the front and back of the panties, to reflect the amount of fabric you feel comfortable wearing.

Problem #3: The amount of elastic at the legs and the waist is uncomfortable—too tight or too loose.

Solution: Remove the stitching and change the length of the elastic to your preference. Make note of the amounts and save them with your pattern for future sewing.

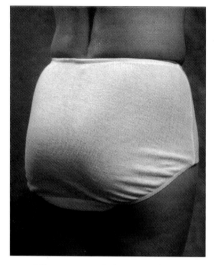

The seat of the panties is baggy.

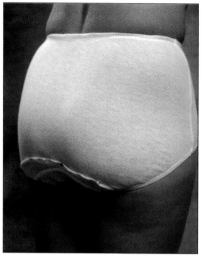

Pin fit the extra fabric in the seat of the panties.

Problem #4: The panties do not fit right at the bottom of your seat! They sag and bag—or, there is not enough fabric in the seat for you to sit comfortably.

Solution: First of all, it is important to check the amount of elastic you have sewn to the legs of the panties. The seat of panties can fit poorly if the elastic is not a good length for your figure. After that step, if the panties are baggy, undo the elastic across the backs of the legs. Try the panties on and reposition the elastic. Mark a smoother and more comfortable location for these elastic sections. A friend is particularly helpful for this task! If the panties ride up at the seat, be sure to check fitting problem #1 first—if the length is a good fit, you may need to add extra length to the pattern in the seat and use that adjustment on your second pair! If the panties are baggy, you may need to shorten the pattern, removing extra fabric.

Center back fold | location of slash line

Straighten the center back fold → Overlap

Straighten the center back fold → Spread

Variations

1. Here is an alternative sewing order for panties:

❖ Sew the front crotch seam.
❖ Sew the back crotch seam.
❖ Sew the two sides seams.
❖ Sew the waist elastic into a circle, and stitch it to the waistline.
❖ Sew the leg elastics into circles and stitch them to the legs.

2. Cover the elastic with a fabric turning technique on the legs of the panties. This method is handy when the colors of the fabric and the elastic are difficult to match, or when you prefer to have fabric next to your skin, instead of elastic.

Trace a pattern from your draft and add a 1/4" (0.6cm) seam allowance to the leg edges, as well as the side seams and crotch seams. Use the guidelines for the amount of elastic as described in step 4 in the detailed construction order. Pin the elastic to the wrong sides of the leg edges. Stitch on the inside edge of elastic, turn the fabric and elastic to the wrong side of the panties, and stitch a second row of zigzag on the inside edge again. This second row of stitching shows on the right side of the panties.

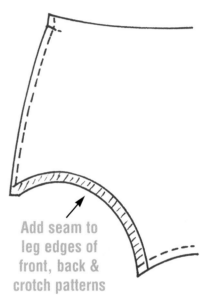

Add seam to leg edges of front, back & crotch patterns

3. Use 5/8" to 1" (1.5cm to 2.5cm) wide elastic stretch lace at the waist. Decide on the amount of stretch lace by trying it around your waist. Mark the edge of the panties and the stretch lace into quarters. Match the quarters, and lap about 1/4" (.6cm) of stretch lace onto edge of panties. Use a zigzag to sew the two layers together. Sew the ends of the stretch lace together when you complete the second side seam.

4. Sew a fabric band to the panties' legs (like a crew neck T-shirt), instead of using elastic. The fabric for the band must be cotton rib knit or cotton interlock, it must have a soft stretch. Cut a band 2" (5cm) wide and about 2" (5cm) shorter in length than the circumference of your leg. Cut off 1/2" (1.3cm) from the entire leg circumference, because this amount will be added onto the panties when the band is sewn into place. Sew a seam in the band, press it open, fold it in half and press lightly. Pin the circular band to the right side of the leg opening, and stitch the three layers together with a 1/4" (.6cm) seam.

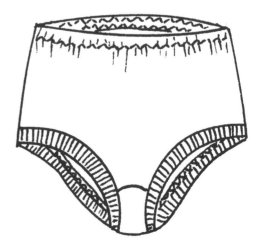

Add a rib knit band at the leg of the panties.

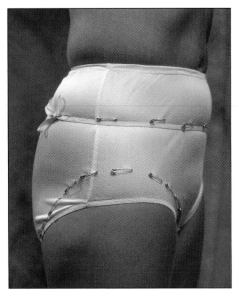

Mark waist and legs.

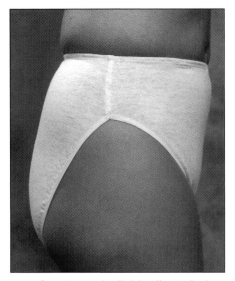

Create an individually styled pair.

5. Create a hipster or bikini style. It is difficult to determine a correct and comfortable location for the top edge of these panties by just measuring the body. For this reason, the test copy of the classic panties is a great tool. Your test panties are the solution to this design challenge because you can tie a piece of narrow elastic around your body at the desired level. With chalk or small safety pins, mark the line you want for hipster or bikini styles on your test panties. Transfer the marks to your paper pattern. Add a seam allowance to the pattern's waist to allow for turning with elastic, and you have created a personalized design.

6. For faster construction and less seaming, lap and pin the paper patterns of the back crotch and back panties. In fabric, cut one front on the fold, a lining crotch from the original pattern and one back on the fold.

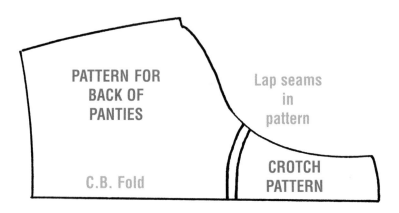

PATTERN FOR
BACK OF
PANTIES

Lap seams
in
pattern

C.B. Fold

CROTCH
PATTERN

To construct:

a) Place the front and back of the panties right sides together, and then place the crotch piece onto the panties' front. Pin together all three layers.

b) Sew the crotch seam.

c) Press the lining crotch toward the back.

d) Zigzag a single edge of the back crotch to the panties.

e) Complete the panties.

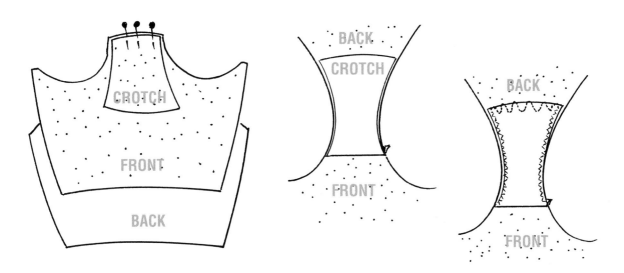

7. For the fastest panties, lap and pin the paper patterns for the front, crotch and back. Cut this entire pattern out in fabric, and cut the crotch again in a soft cotton knit for a lining. Lay the crotch on the wrong side of the panties and multiple zigzag it into place. Sew the elastic to the leg edges. Sew one side seam. Sew the elastic to the waist, and then sew the second side seam.

Grid Pattern for Classic Panties

This is a half scale grid drawing of the Classic Pantie pattern. Side and crotch seam allowances of 1/4" (0.6cm) are included in the pattern.

The legs have no seam allowances, as they are intended to be finished with the lapping of elastic method described in step 4 of the Classic Panties Construction. The waist edge has a 3/8" (1cm) turning allowance for elastic.

You can make the full scale pattern in one of two ways:

1. Use a photocopier: Set the copier to x200, place this book into the machine and make a copy. The patterns will fit onto 11" x 17" paper. The pattern has grain lines and fold lines and is ready for layout and cutting.

2. Draw the pattern onto 1" (2.5cm) grid paper. One square on the grid equals 1" (2.5cm). Count out the squares to draw the basic shape of the pattern first, and then draw curves and shapes using a curved ruler, along with the grid, as your guide.

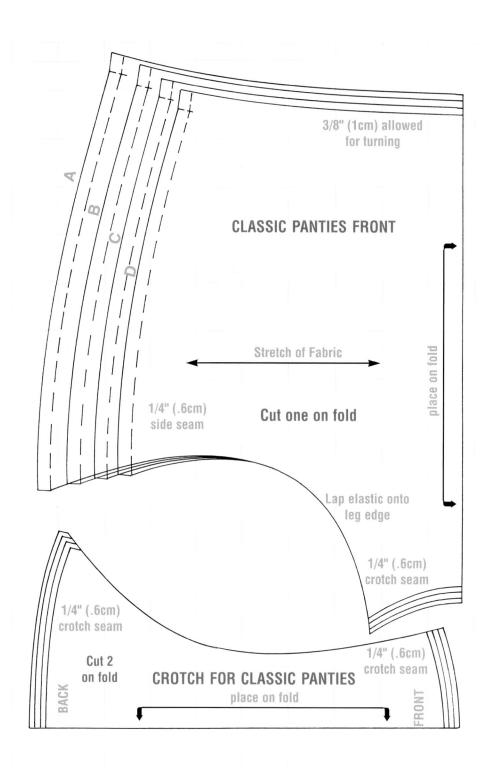

A
B
C
D

3/8" (1cm) allowed
for turning

CLASSIC PANTIES FRONT

Stretch of Fabric

place on fold

1/4" (.6cm)
side seam

Cut one on fold

Lap elastic onto
leg edge

1/4" (.6cm)
crotch seam

1/4" (.6cm)
crotch seam

1/4" (.6cm)
crotch seam

BACK

Cut 2
on fold

CROTCH FOR CLASSIC PANTIES

place on fold

FRONT

A. Hip 41" to 43" (104cm to 109cm)
B. Hip 38" to 40" (96cm to 101cm)
C. Hip 38" to 40" (96cm to 101cm)
D. Hip 34" to 35" (86cm to 89cm)

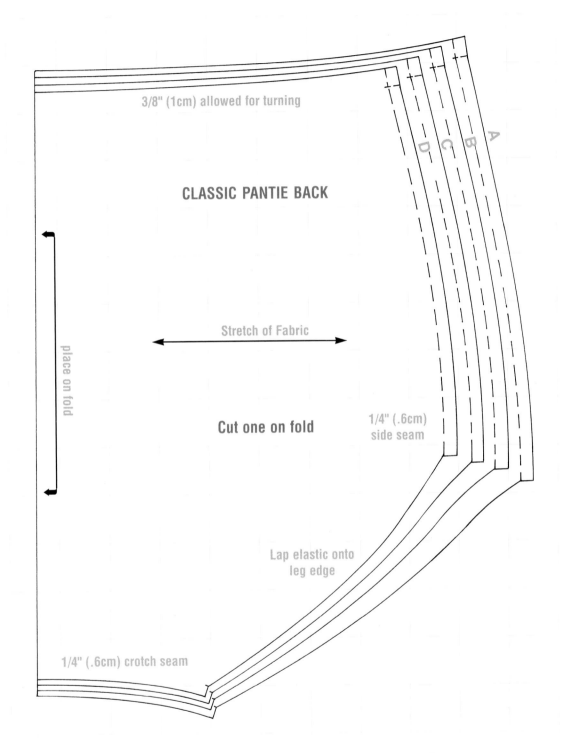

3/8" (1cm) allowed for turning

CLASSIC PANTIE BACK

Stretch of Fabric

place on fold

Cut one on fold

1/4" (.6cm)
side seam

Lap elastic onto
leg edge

1/4" (.6cm) crotch seam

A. Hip 41" to 43" (104cm to 109cm)
B. Hip 38" to 40" (96cm to 101cm)
C. Hip 38" to 40" (96cm to 101cm)
D. Hip 34" to 35" (86cm to 89cm)

Chapter 9

Specialty Designs

Attractive colors and interesting fabric textures enhance the appeal of all clothing designs. We often think of these things first and yet, functional design may be even more important. The wonderful aspect of sewing is that a personalized, functional design can combine with your personal color and fabric preferences to make a truly functional, unique garment!

Special occasions in our lives call for special designs. Attractive, comfortable panties during pregnancy are a treat for the wearer. A pretty nursing nightie design will be a welcome addition to a new mother's wardrobe.

Easy Dressing Ideas introduces the basics of developing practical and thoughtful solutions for some of the unique physical challenges some women have. Functional designs need to also be attractive. The ideas for the knit nightie and the half slip are especially welcome, because they are simple to sew and simple to wear!

Maternity Panties

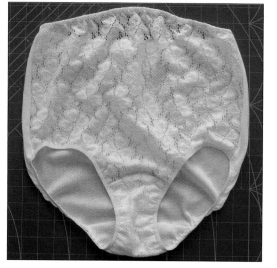

The panties are sewn in exactly the same way as has been described for Classic Panties. The difference is in the fabric selection. The front of the maternity panties must be cut in two-way stretch fabric. The fabric might be nylon stretch lace, cotton/spandex or other fabrics you enjoy. These two-way stretch fabrics allow a comfortable fit as the body changes during pregnancy. The back of the panties could be cotton single knit or nylon tricot, or two-way stretch fabric.

The waist can be sewn as a casing, to allow flexibility in the size of the panties, or by sewing the elastic permanently into place. See page 73, Chapter 6 for casing construction directions.

The leg edges have no allowance for turning. Use the lapping method for elastic application.

The grid drawing of the Maternity Panties pattern is included here in half scale. Seam allowances of 1/4" (0.6cm) for the sides and crotch are included in the pattern, and a turning allowance of 3/8" (1cm) has been included at the waist. You can make the full scale pattern in one of two ways:

1. Use a photocopier: Set the copier to x200, place this book into the machine and make a copy. The patterns fit onto 11" x 17" paper. The pattern has grain lines and fold lines, and is ready for layout and cutting.

2. Draw the pattern onto 1" grid paper. One square on the grid equals 1" (2.5cm). Count out the squares to draw the basic shape of the pattern first, and then draw curves and shapes using a curved ruler, along with the grid, as your guide.

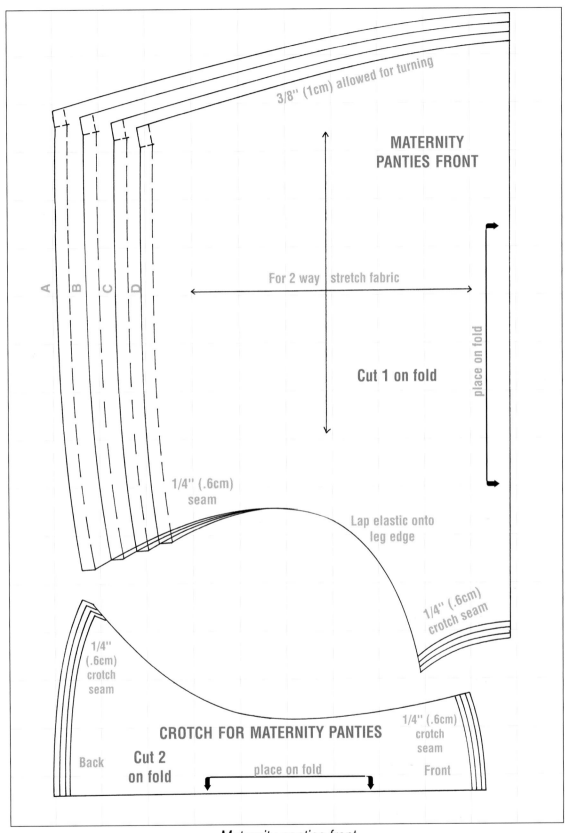

3/8" (1cm) allowed for turning

**MATERNITY
PANTIES FRONT**

For 2 way stretch fabric

place on fold

Cut 1 on fold

1/4" (.6cm)
seam

Lap elastic onto
leg edge

1/4" (.6cm)
crotch seam

1/4"
(.6cm)
crotch
seam

1/4" (.6cm)
crotch
seam

CROTCH FOR MATERNITY PANTIES

Back

**Cut 2
on fold**

place on fold

Front

A B C D

Maternity panties front.

A. Hip 41" to 43" (104cm to 109cm)   C. Hip 36" to 37" (91cm to 94cm)
B. Hip 38" to 40" (96cm to 101 cm)   D. Hip 34" to 35" (86cm to 89cm)

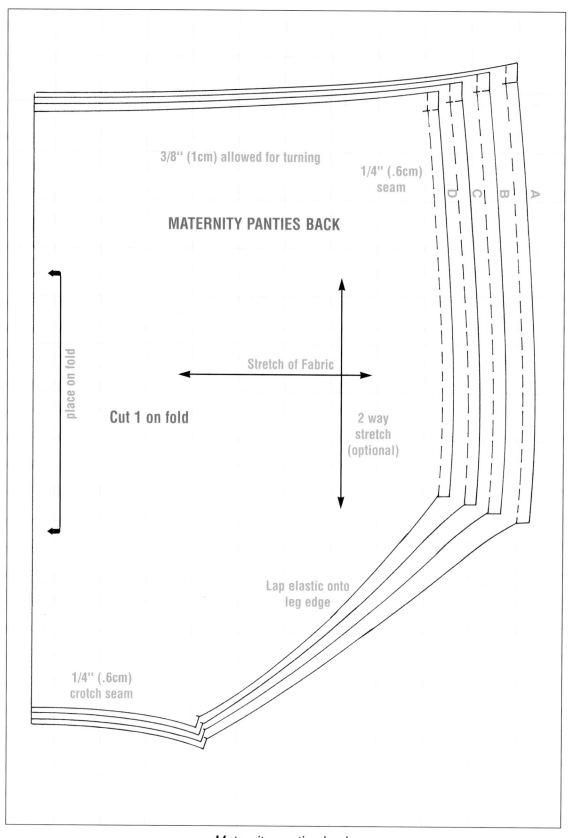

3/8" (1cm) allowed for turning

1/4" (.6cm) seam

MATERNITY PANTIES BACK

D C B A

place on fold

Stretch of Fabric

2 way stretch (optional)

Cut 1 on fold

Lap elastic onto leg edge

1/4" (.6cm) crotch seam

Maternity panties back.

A. Hip 41" to 43" (104cm to 109cm)   C. Hip 36" to 37" (91cm to 94cm)
B. Hip 38" to 40" (96cm to 101 cm)   D. Hip 34" to 35" (86cm to 89cm)

Fabric Required

1/2 yard (0.5M) of each—the stretch lace for front, and another knit for the back. This makes enough for two pairs.

Layout

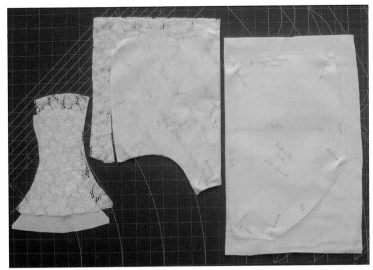

Layout of the maternity panties.

Detailed Sewing Order:

Please follow the sewing order for the Classic Panties in Chapter 8, beginning on page 92.

Nursing Nightie

Begin with a roomy shirt, blouse or dress pattern and add the pleats. The purpose of the pleats is to offer the nursing mother a convenient, attractive, functional design. Two pleats are added to the front of your existing nightie pattern. Each pleat is sewn together in the upper section of the body and in the area below the bust. The pleats fall softly to the hem. The inside fold line of the pleat is cut open, and the raw edge is neatly finished. The opening provides easy access to the breast for nursing.

The pleat detail could also be added below a bodice yoke design, so check through your stash of patterns and create something wonderful!

Redesign an existing pattern to create the Nursing Nightie by using the following steps:

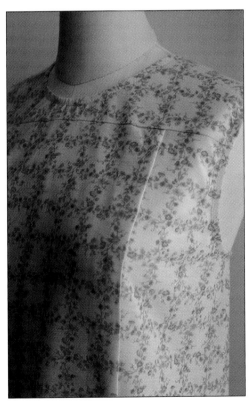

The pleat conceals an open front for nursing.

1. Select an easy or loose fitting pattern. You can determine the ease in a garment by reading the pattern company's description on the back of the pattern envelope. It could be for a blouse, top, dress or nightie. Your bust measurement is the basis for size selection. The pattern's length may be thigh, knee or floor.

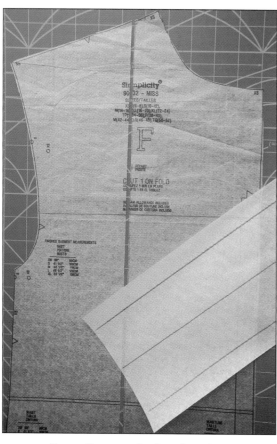
Draw lines to design the pleat.

2. Draw line A on the pattern. The line must be parallel to the center front, and drawn the length of the pattern. Use this guide to determine the distance you need to place this line from the center front:

5" (12.7cm) for bust sizes 32" to 35" (81cm to 89cm)

5-1/2" (14cm) for bust sizes 36" to 41"(91cm to104cm)

6" (15.4cm) for bust sizes 42" to 44" (107cm to 112cm)

Line A ends up on the shoulder line for most patterns. The exception is on a pattern with a wide bateau neckline—then line A may begin in the neckline area of your pattern.

3. In the upper bodice area, square line B from the center front, over to the armhole or side seam of the pattern. This is not to mark a specific place on your pattern—this guideline is only needed to check alignment later on. It is not a sewing line. There should be a waist-line mark on your pattern, usually on the center front line. Extend this waistline marking from the center front to the side seam.

4. On another piece of pattern paper draw three lines, 2" (5cm) apart and parallel to one another. The lines need to be at least as long as your pattern. Label the lines as 1, 2 and 3.

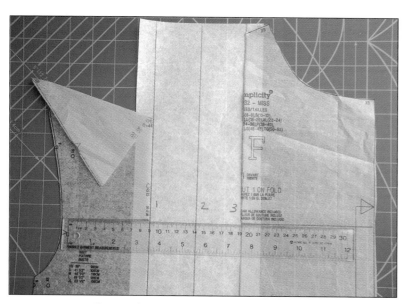
Cut and spread the pattern, and add paper with #1, #2, and #3 pleat lines.

5. Cut your pattern apart on line A from hem to shoulder. Spread the pattern apart and place the paper with three parallel lines in the space.

6. Align lines 1 and 3 along the two cut pattern edges (what was line A). Lay a ruler on line B to check whether your pattern is level.

7. Tape the pattern together.

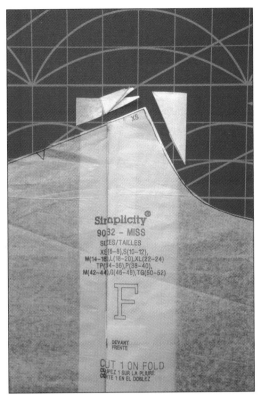

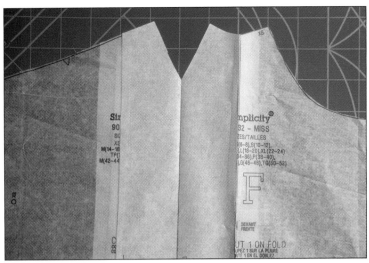

The pattern shape with the pleat.

Fold the pleat and true up the shoulder and neck edges.

8. Fold the pattern on line 3 and match it up to line 1. The fold of the pleat must go toward the center front of your pattern. With the fold in place, cut off the excess paper around the neckline and the shoulder line, to true up the top edge of the pleat and make for accurate sewing.

You can also design a front yoke and pleat:

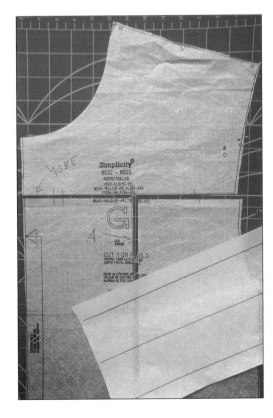

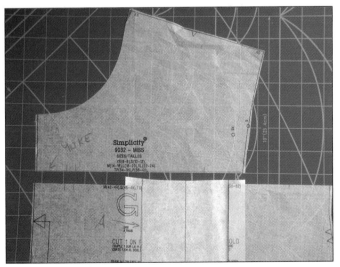

Design a yoke and pleat.

Jan Bones

Fabric Required

This adaptation of an existing pattern is suitable for knit or woven fabrics. Follow the pattern's fabric suggestions, and use the pattern's directions and diagrams for layout and cutting.

> *Tip*: The front pattern is 8" (20.4cm) wider because of the pleat detail, so you may well need to buy additional fabric.

Detailed Sewing Order for the Nursing Nightie

1. Mark the pleat lines 1, 2, and 3 on the fabric. Use marking pencil, wheel and carbon or any marking method you prefer.

2. Fold each of the two pleats right sides together. Match lines 1 and 3 and pin. Beginning at shoulder, permanently stitch 5" to 7" down the pinned line (10cm to 15.4cm). Machine baste the rest of the pleat line to hem of the garment piece.

> *Tip*: The length of the stitching line varies according to your overall height, the distance from your breast to shoulder and your size.

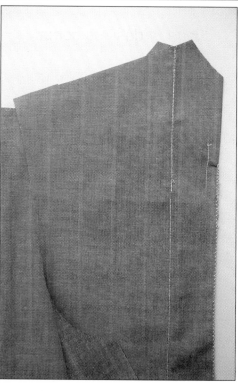

Mark, sew and fold pleats.

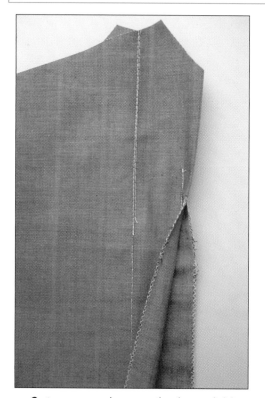

Cut open and serge the inner fold.

3. Cut a slash on the fold of the pleat. Begin cutting 2" to 3" (5cm to 7.5cm) up from the waist marking on pattern and stop cutting 1" (2.5cm) above the stitching line completed in step 3.

4. Finish these raw edges by serging or zigzagging. When serging, move the knife or avoid using it, because the fabric must not be cut away. If you use a zigzag, let the right side of the stitch go over the raw edge, and left side of stitch go into the fabric. This makes a neat, no-bulk finish.

5. To secure the ends of the slash and to keep the inner fold of the pleat lying smoothly, stitch 3/4" (2cm) above and below the end of the slash, 3/8" (1cm) away from the fold.

6. Sew along the neck and/or shoulder to hold the ends of the pleat to the front of the design.

7. Continue the construction of the garment, following the pattern instructions and diagrams.

Easy Dressing Knit Nightie or Camisole

Lingerie designs commonly slip over the head. This may prove to be difficult for some women. Our range of motion changes as we age, and illness or injury can prevent the arms from lifting above the head. Front-closing designs are a great solution.

This design idea is a variation of the Knit Camisole and Nightie in Chapter 5. For an Easy Dressing design, add a button closure to the front of the camisole or nightie. The size of the button can be large or small, depending on the dexterity of the wearer. Snap tape is twill tape with snaps already riveted in place. It often is available in white or black. If those colors suit your fabric, this product could be used. If not, select matching satin ribbon and buttons. Hook-and-loop fasteners can add convenience as well. (Note: Care must be taken with hook-and-loop fasteners, such as Velcro®. They must be backed completely by fabric, because they feel rough against the skin. Also, when laundering, safety pin the hook-and-loop sides together, to prevent the hook side's snagging other fabrics.)

To make the design, follow these steps:

❖ Cut the pattern for the camisole skirt in fabric, and cut along the centerline to make two front pieces. Also cut the bodice pieces, and trim off the center front seam allowance.

❖ Sew the nightie together, leaving the entire front edge open.

❖ Sew a row of gathering stitches along the center front edge of the bodice, and pull the threads until the edge measures:
3" (7.5cm) for bust sizes 32"-33" and 34"-35"
3-1/2" (9cm) for bust sizes 36"-38" and 39"-41"
4" (10.2cm) for bust size 42"-44"

Cut open and serge the inner fold.

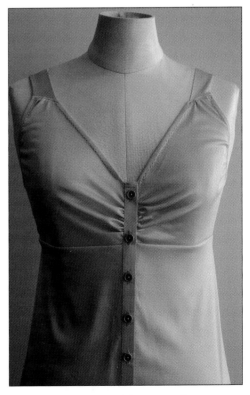

An open front with snap closures makes this slip easy to wear.

❖ You now need two lengths of satin ribbon or snap tape, 3/4" to 1" (2cm-2.5cm) wide, one for the left side and one for the right side. Cut the ribbon 3/4" (2cm) longer than the front edge. Lap the ribbon onto the right side of the fabric by about 1/4" (0.6cm). Leave 3/8" (1cm) extra at the neck and hem. Fold the extra ends to the wrong side of the camisole. The snap tape is best sewn into place with a zipper foot.

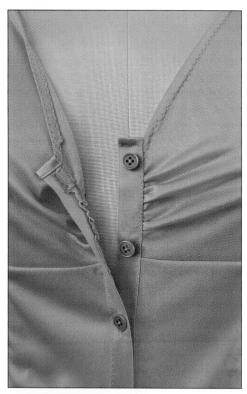 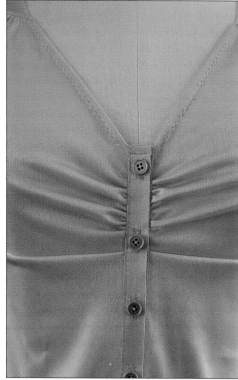

❖ Sew along the very edge of the ribbon or tape and join it to the camisole. Use a straight stitch or narrow zigzag. Make vertical buttonholes on the right side, and sew buttons on the left side of the ribbon.

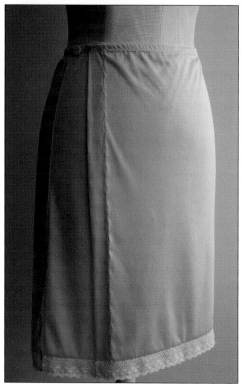

Easy Dressing Half Slip

Stepping into clothing is automatic for many of us. Skirts, pantyhose and dress pants require that we lean over and lift one leg while stretching our arms out to pull the clothing onto our body. This is not always a simple task. A garment that can simply be wrapped around the body offers a great "easy dressing" solution to this obstacle. Fabric choice can further customize this slip design, because different fabrics can address different needs. Thin, lightweight cotton knit feels cool. Clothing glides easily over nylon tricot. Polyester interlock drapes nicely over the body. The bias cutting direction on a woven fabric also works well. See Variation 2, page 73 in Chapter 6.

A simple wrap half slip is made from the slip in Chapter 5. For this slip you need fabric, two buttons, satin ribbon and lace (optional). Here is how to make this design:

❖ The back slip pattern is used as it is.

❖ Begin with a folded piece of pattern paper and trace the front slip. Cut the pattern out—and when the paper is unfolded, you will have the entire front. On this paper pattern, measure 3" to 4" (7.5 to 10cm) from one side seam and draw a straight line from the waist to the hem (cut the extra paper away). This line is parallel to the center front.

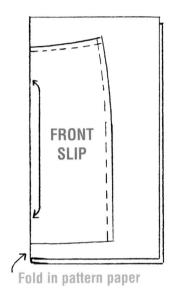

FRONT SLIP

FRONT SLIP

Fold in pattern paper

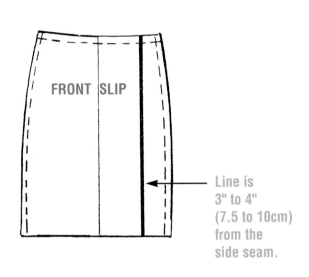

FRONT SLIP

Line is 3" to 4" (7.5 to 10cm) from the side seam.

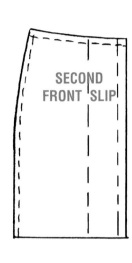

SECOND FRONT SLIP

❖ In fabric, cut one back on the fold and cut two fronts.

❖ Sew the side seams.

❖ Turn under and stitch 1" (2.5cm) along the long straight edges on the fronts.

❖ Sew elastic to the entire waist edge.

❖ Sew loops of satin ribbon to the corners of the slip's waist. Make the loop fit the button. The right side of the slip, when worn, laps over the left. Sew one button on the right side of the fabric, on the right front slip. Sew the second button on the wrong side of the fabric on the left front.

> **Tip**: If you love the look of the six-panel slip, it could be a wrap too! Cut nine panels and eight godets and follow the same ideas outlined for the half slip.

Loop and button on waist of slip.

Chapter 10

Boxers

Today's boxers are a truly popular design, worn by a large cross section of people. Traditionally worn by men as underwear, boxers have come a long way! Now, they are sometimes made in silk to match a beautiful camisole for the bride-to-be. For teenagers, boxers may be cotton plaid with a designer's name on the elastic waistband—and for everyone else boxers could be flannelette, cotton knit, tricot or fleece.

The great thing about boxers is the variety. Almost any knit or woven fabric can be used. The boxers may be any length. They might have a fly front for men. They are sometimes made to be tight fitting, and sometimes baggy—and there are options for finishing at the waist.

The basic boxer is a simple sewing project, excellent for the novice sewer. As more design details are added, the project becomes more complicated, so you have the opportunity to choose the level of sewing, and to advance your own capabilities.

One easy way to create a boxer pattern is to redesign an existing pattern. Select a basic commercial pattern for pant or shorts. It is fine if there are pre-existing details on the pattern, such as darts and a waistband. These details are altered to simplify the pattern.

The technique described here works for children's sizes and adult sizes alike. Measure the hip size of the body and use that measurement as the guide for selecting a pattern. There is often extra tissue around the commercial pattern—leave it and use it for the new lines of the boxer. Because the boxer silhouette is simple, it is workable to use a ladies' pattern to create a teenage boy or man's boxer—just keep it a secret!

Redesign an existing pattern to create the "No-Side-Seam Boxer."
Follow these steps:

1. Draw the existing straight of grain line on the front and back pattern pieces, up to the waist area.

2. If there is a "shorten or lengthen" line drawn across front and back patterns, draw over these lines in red pencil. If there is no "shorten or lengthen" line, draw a red line at right angles to the grain line. Draw this line just above the crotch curve.

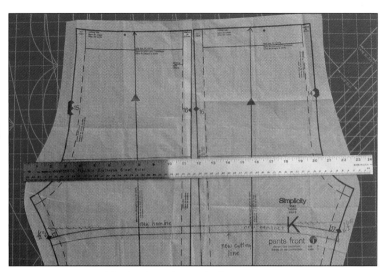

Redesign the existing pattern.

3. Place the front and back pant patterns side by side. The two straight of grain lines must be parallel to each other. For lines to be parallel, they must be equal in their distance apart for their entire length. At the same time as the grain lines are parallel, the crosswise red lines must create a continuous straight line across the two patterns.

4. The amount of ease in the boxers is determined by the ease of the original pattern, and by how closely you place the two patterns. You may line up the side seam lines of the front and back, or you may add ease by keeping the seam lines apart slightly. Plan to have the ease in the range of 2" to 6" (5cm to 15.4cm). If you are making the boxers in a knit fabric, less ease is necessary because the stretch of the fabric adds comfort. If a woven fabric is selected, the ease needs to be more generous.

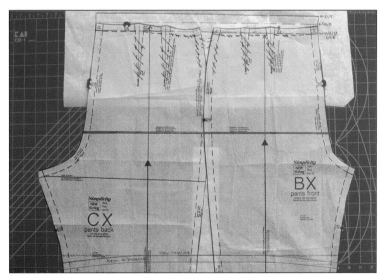

Line up the side seams, or leave some space to add ease.

5. To redesign the waistline, you have three options:

a) If you want to simply lap the elastic onto the waist of the boxer, so the elastic is showing, follow these steps:

❖ If the original pattern you are using has darts, cross them out and draw a new, straight waistline from the center front to center back.

❖ Add 3/8" (1cm) seam allowance above this new waistline. This small allowance is used when the elastic is lapped onto the boxer.

b) If you want to enclose and hide the elastic within a fold of fabric at the waist, draw a line 2" (5cm) above and parallel to the new waistline. This is the amount needed to sew 1" elastic into the waist.

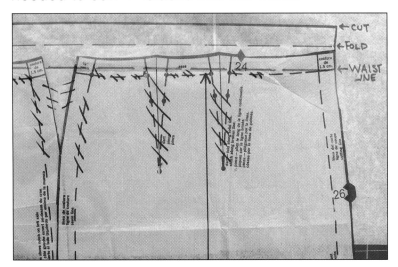

c) The pattern you are redesigning may already have an allowance for enclosing the elastic. Check the width—it needs to be double the width of the elastic you wish to use.

Allowance for the enclosed elastic.

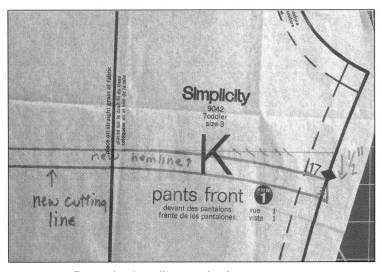

Draw the hemline on the boxer pattern.

6. Draw the hemline of boxer. Determine the length you wish to have for the completed garment. Measure down the side area of the pattern and mark the desired length. From that point, draw a line across the pattern, parallel to the red line. To prevent the boxers from creeping up between the legs while walking, some shape needs to be added. Measure down 1/2" (1.3cm) below the hemline, on the front inseam and the back inseam. From that point, draw a very gradual curve, about 8" (20.4cm) long in an adult-sized pattern, to the hemline. For the best sewing results, the junction of the hem and the inside leg seam should be square.

7. Seam allowances at the inside leg seam and crotch seam are 5/8" (1.5cm) on the commercial pattern. Leave this amount if you wish to sew the boxers with a French seam finish. If you are sewing on a serger, you will be able to align the raw edges to the 5/8" (1.5cm) line on the serger and then cut off the extra with the knife. If you are sewing with a regular machine, you might change the seam to 3/8" (1cm) to reduce bulk.

8. Add a 3/8" (1cm) hem allowance to the leg edge.

Fabric Required

The boxer length and size determines the fabric needed. A good general rule to follow is two times the boxer pattern length, plus 4" (10.2cm) for shrinkage and straightening. Some fabrics are wide enough for both pieces to be cut from one length. This is the case with children's patterns.

Boxers for children may often be cut from fabric in the same length as the pattern.

A fabric width of 1-1/8 yd (1M) of 45" (115cm) works for most adult sizes.

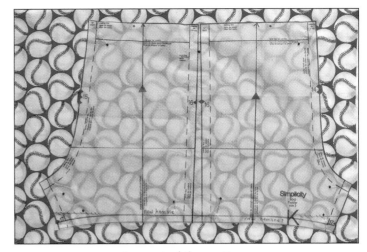

Layout of the pattern.

Layout

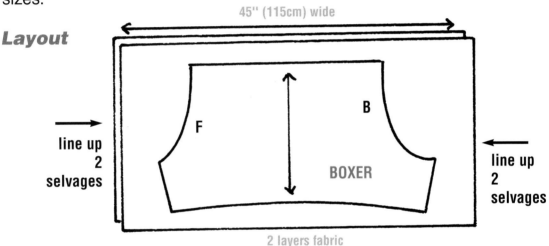

45" (115cm) wide

line up 2 selvages

F

B

BOXER

line up 2 selvages

2 layers fabric

Detailed Sewing Order for the Boxer

1. To sew an inside leg seam, place front and back right side together, and serge or stitch on a regular sewing machine.

2. A French seam is an excellent method for the boxers inside leg seam, too. It creates a durable seam, and all the raw edges of the fabric are enclosed. Follow these steps:

a) Place the two seam edges wrong sides together, and sew a 1/4" (0.6cm) seam.

b) Fold the same seam edges, now placing them right sides together. Sew a 3/8" (1cm) seam. Press the seam allowances toward the back of the garment, and the seam is complete.

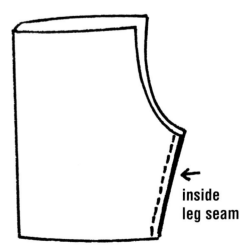

inside leg seam

Sew the inside leg seams of the boxers.

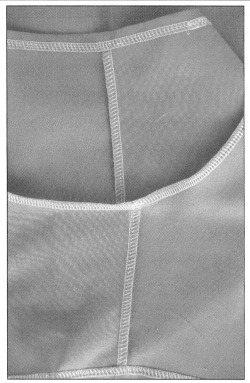

Press the inside leg seams in opposite directions to reduce bulk.

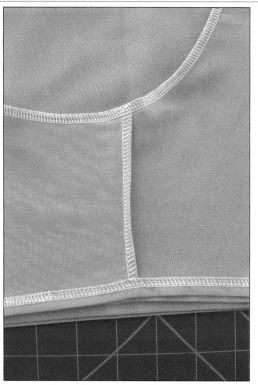

Sew the crotch seams with a serger.

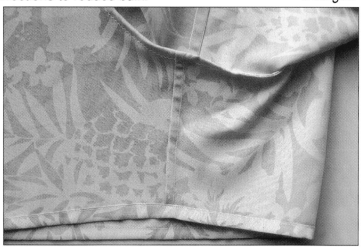

Sew the crotch seams together with a French seam.

3. Sew the crotch seam. To do this, have one leg right side out and one leg wrong side out. This way, you can put one leg inside the other, right sides together. Stitching is easy because the entire seam is visible. Use the serger or the regular sewing machine to sew this seam, or, because the crotch seam curve is long and gradual, the French seam is a great alternative for lightweight fabric. Follow the directions in step 2.

4. Waist elastic for a boxer is usually 1" (2.5cm) in width. To begin, sew your elastic into a circle by butting the ends together and zigzagging over them. Mark the top edge of boxers and the elastic into quarters with pins.

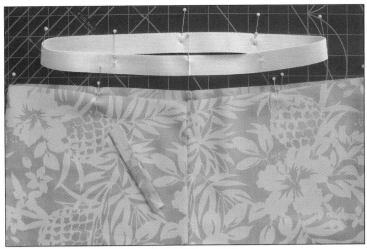

Sew the elastic into a circle, mark the elastic and the boxers into quarters or eighths.

Tip: Marking the boxer and the elastic into eight equal parts makes for easier sewing. The more you pin, the greater control you have — just remember to remove the pins as you work around the waist, so that you do not sew over them.

Select one of the following five methods for applying elastic:

The overlap method for elastic.

a) Overlap method:

❖ For woven fabrics, serge or zigzag the waist edge to prevent fraying. For knits, no finish is needed, because the fabric does not ravel.

❖ Lap the elastic onto the right side of the waist edge of the boxer by 3/8" (1cm). Match the quarter pin markings and pin the elastic to the boxer.

❖ Place a 4" (10.2cm) long piece of 1/2" (1.3cm) wide ribbon between the elastic and the right side of the boxer at the elastic's join.

❖ Stretch the elastic to fit the waist edge of the boxer and use a plain, medium width zigzag to sew the two layers together, along the lower edge of the elastic. Allow the left side of the zigzag to sew over the elastic edge into the fabric, and the right side of the zigzag into the elastic.

❖ Wrap the ribbon to inside of the boxer and sew a square of stitching along the edge of ribbon. This finishes the join.

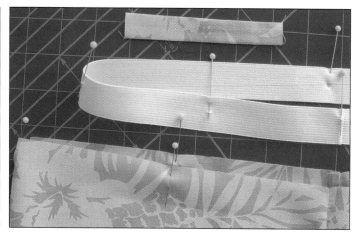

Use a piece of self fabric for the cover of the elastic join.

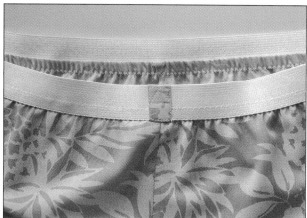

Overlapped and exposed methods for elastic.

b) Exposed elastic method: This is a good method for lightweight woven fabrics. Use 1" (2.5cm) wide elastic. It seems to be a very backward way to sew elastic, but the results are great. I like to use the medium width zigzag for this sewing method. Straight stitching could also be used. The steps:

❖ Place the elastic on the wrong side of the boxer waist edge. The elastic must extend only 1/4" (0.6cm) above the top of the boxer.

❖ Stretch the elastic and sew down the center of the elastic to join it to the boxer. That would be 1/2" (1.3cm) away from elastic's edge.

❖ Turn the elastic to the right side of the boxer.

❖ Sew on the lower edge of the elastic.

c) Covered elastic method: This method is good for lightweight fabric. It is also helpful when the elastic color does not suit the fabric. Note: For this method, the pattern must have a 2" allowance above the waistline. The steps:

❖ Pin the elastic to the wrong side of the boxer, with the top edge of the elastic lined up to top edge of the boxer.

❖ Zigzag along the lower edge of the elastic.

❖ Turn the elastic and the fabric to the wrong side.

Covered method for elastic.

❖ Sew on the lower edge again, this time sewing through the fabric and the elastic. This row of stitching shows on the right side of the garment.

d) A casing is also possible for the boxer. This is an excellent method for people who fluctuate in weight, or if you are making a gift, and the exact size is not known.

❖ Use 3/4" (2cm) wide elastic. Make a 3/4" vertical machine buttonhole beside the center back seam.

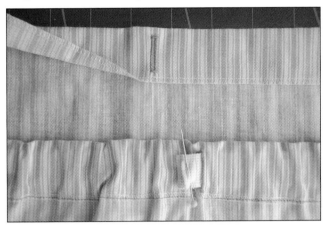

Casing for the elastic.

> **Tip**: When you are using a knit, stabilize the area first by pressing a small strip of iron-on interfacing where the buttonhole is to be located. Then cut the buttonhole open.

❖ Turn down and press to the inside 1" (2.5cm) of fabric at the boxer's waist edge. Stitch it into place. Use a regular straight stitch or a slight zigzag, or sew from the right side with a twin needle.

❖ The elastic may now be run through the casing using the buttonhole opening and there is always easy access to the elastic if its size needs to be changed.

e) To make a casing at the waist with even more flexibility than elastic, try this:

❖ Cut a 24" cotton shoelace in half.

❖ Decide on the normal length of elastic for the waist and then subtract 6" (15.4cm). Cut the elastic according to this shorter length.

❖ Sew one piece of the shoelace to each end of the elastic with a medium width zigzag stitch.

❖ Thread the elastic/shoelace through the casing.

❖ Sew the elastic to the waist of the boxer at the center back. This prevents the elastic and shoelace from pulling out of the casing.

5. Hem the leg edges: Serge or zigzag the raw edges, turn 3/8" (1cm) to the wrong side, and topstitch close to the raw edges. Or, you might double-turn the raw edges and topstitch.

Variation

Create a fly front for the boxer:

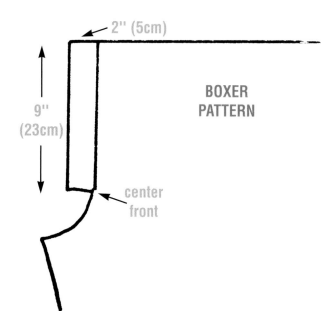

Plaid fly front boxers.

Draw a 2" by 9" (5cm by 23cm) section onto the boxer pattern front seam. This is the fly facing. Lay the pattern on fabric, and cut the boxer with the fly facing.

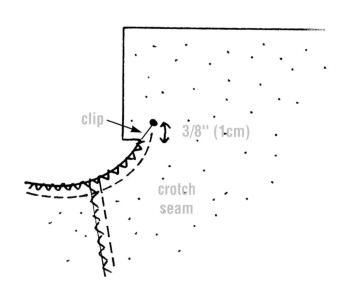

Follow the sewing directions for the boxer, and when stitching the crotch seam, stop 3/8" (1cm) above the bottom of the fly facing. Clip into the end of the stitching.

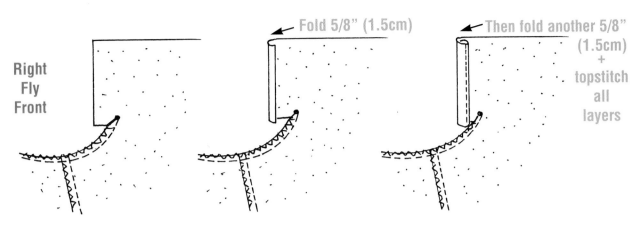

Right Fly Front

Fold 5/8" (1.5cm)

Then fold another 5/8" (1.5cm) + topstitch all layers

For men's boxers, the left fly front laps over the right fly front. On the right fly front, fold 5/8" (1.5cm) to the wrong side of the fly and press. Then fold another 5/8" (1.5cm) to the wrong side, and top stitch close to the inside edge.

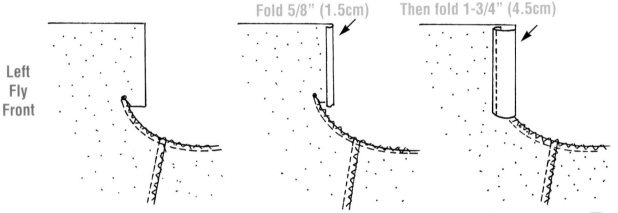

Left Fly Front

Fold 5/8" (1.5cm)

Then fold 1-3/4" (4.5cm)

On the left fly front, fold 5/8" (1.5cm) to wrong side of the fly and press. Then fold another 1-3/4" (4.5cm) to the wrong side and press.

The left fly laps over the right fly by 1-1/4" (3cm). Topstitch along the edge of the left front fly facing. Turn the corner at the bottom of the facing and continue stitching to the center front seam. When sewing across the bottom, attach both the left and right facings to the boxers. Sew all the layers of the fly together at the waist edge, and add a button and buttonhole on the fly front. Continue with the sewing directions to complete the boxers.

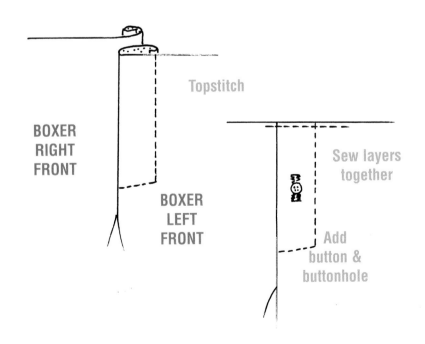

Topstitch

BOXER RIGHT FRONT

BOXER LEFT FRONT

Sew layers together

Add button & buttonhole

Chapter 11

Lingerie Roll

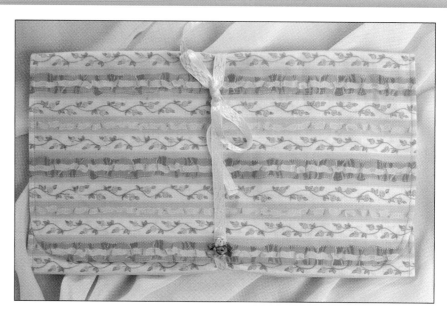

C all it the Pantie Pouch, the Sexy Stash or the Bra Bag! By any name, this design is practical for storage, great for travel and terrific as a gift. The wide variety of fabric choices—polyester satin, cotton eyelet and silk brocade—are only the beginning. The roll is held closed with satin ribbon or self fabric tie.

Supplies required

❖ 15" (0.4M) of 60" (150cm) wide fabric, or 30" (0.8M) of 45" (115cm) wide fabric
❖ 3 lightweight, 12" (30cm) long zippers
❖ Thread
❖ 1 yard (0.9M) any width ribbon or fancy cord.
❖ 1/3 yard (0.3M) of 1/8" (0.3cm) ribbon

Prepare and Mark the Fabric

1. Cut two rectangles from the selected fabric, measuring 15" x 30" (38cm x 76cm).

2. Work from the wrong side of fabric. Along the two long edges, measure up from the bottom and mark at the points 8", 16" and 24" (20.4cm, 40.7cm and 61cm). Lay a ruler across fabric, match the marks and draw three lines across the rectangle.

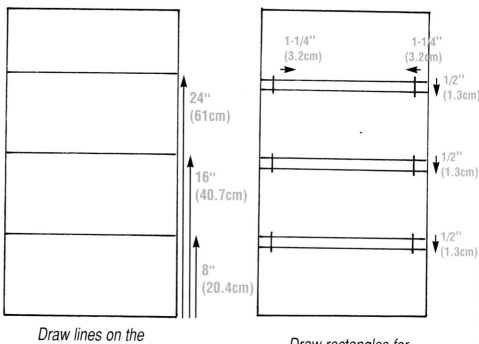

Draw lines on the lingerie roll.

Draw rectangles for zipper locations.

3. Draw a second line 1/2" (1.3cm) below each of the three lines.

4. Measure in 1-1/4" (3.2cm) from the long edges, and draw short lines at each of the three pairs of lines. These three rectangles are the zipper pocket locations.

Tip: The layout of the lingerie roll on fabric makes for easy sewing because the short edges of the rectangle are on the fabric's straight of grain. The openings for the zippers will be easily stitched and pressed with this grain direction.

Detailed Sewing Order

Use a reinforcing stitch around the rectangles for the zippers.

1. Sew zippers into place:

Using a short straight stitch (approximately15-18 stitches per inch), sew around the rectangles drawn on the wrong side of the fabric. As you sew, carefully and accurately pivot and turn at the rectangle's corners.

Cut down the center of the rectangle. About 1/2" (1.3cm) from each end, cut into the corners.

Serge or zigzag the raw edges and press.

Serge or zigzag the two long edges made when the rectangle was cut down the center. This step ensures that the threads do not become entangled in the zipper teeth.

Lay the fabric on the ironing board with wrong side facing you. Fold the long edges and the ends of the rectangle to the wrong side and press well. The stitching line is the guide—the fabric will fold easily along this line.

Lay the lingerie roll with its right side facing you and position the three zippers into the three openings.

Stitch the zippers into place by sewing as close to the edge of the rectangle as you can. This operation is most easily completed with a zipper presser foot.

2. Unzip one zipper. This will be the opening for turning the roll.

3. With the right sides together, lay the two rectangles together.

4. Sew around the entire circumference of the two layers of the roll. Follow the fabric edges as they were originally cut, and sew the corners as squares—or round all four corners slightly and sew curves. Sew and trim all raw edges to an even 1/4" (0.6cm), or serge the edges.

5. Turn the roll right side out through the opened zipper, press carefully and topstitch around the circumference with a 3/8" (1cm) seam. The topstitching is an important step, because it encloses all the seam allowances.

Position the zippers into the rectangles and stitch.

Round the corners

or keep them square

Sew around the entire lingerie roll.

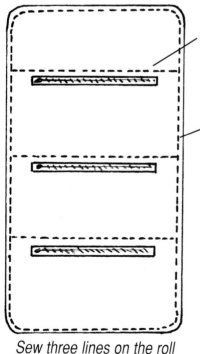

topstitch 3 lines to create pockets

topstitch the edge

Sew three lines on the roll to create pockets.

6. Sew three lines of topstitching across the lingerie roll. These lines divide the roll into pockets. Stitch 1/4" (0.6cm) above each of the three zippers, and sew through two layers of fabric.

Tie narrow ribbons to the zipper pulls.

7. Cut the 1/3yd (0.3M) narrow ribbon into three pieces. Slip each piece through the zipper pulls, and tie. This makes for easy access into the pockets of the lingerie roll.

8. Place the center of the 1-yard length of ribbon at the middle of the top edge of the lingerie roll. Note that the top flap of the roll is the area of fabric measuring 6" (15cm) from the edge of the zipper to the raw edge of the fabric. Stitch the ribbon to the lingerie roll.

Sew the ribbon at the center of the lingerie roll's top edge.

Variations

1. Cut one rectangle in sheer organza to make lingerie easier to locate.

2. Add as many extra pockets as you like. They could be patch pockets made as squares or rectangles, sewn in the space between the zippers. They could be closed at their tops with snaps, buttons and buttonholes or ties.

3. Before sewing the rectangles together, decorate the flap of the roll with machine embroidery, machine-stitched initials, appliquéd lace and any other fun details appropriate to the fabric.

4. Adjust the size of the lingerie roll according to your taste, the items being packed, or the amount of fabric available.

5. For a lingerie roll that can hang, plan the shape of flap section of roll to duplicate shape of a flat wooden hanger. Follow the first five steps of directions; just remember to leave a 2" (2.5cm) opening at center of flap when stitching the two layers together. Then before step 6 is completed, place the hanger inside the roll and lead the hook of hanger through the opening.

Tack the two layers of the roll together under the hanger. Do this by hand or by machine. This prevents the hanger's moving out of position.

Draw and cut the top of the roll to fit the hanger shape.

6. Make a lingerie roll to coordinate with a nightie or sleep set, for a lovely gift.

Jan Bones

Index

PRACTICAL PROJECTS THAT WILL INSPIRE NOVICE AND EXPERT SEWERS ALIKE

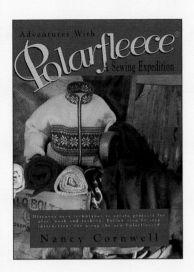

Adventures with Polarfleece®
A Sewing Expedition
by Nancy Cornwell
Nancy Cornwell will lead you on a sewing expedition. Explore and discover endless project possibilities for the entire family. Sew a collection of 15 projects for play, work, fashion, comfort and warmth. The heart of a fallen-away sewer will soon be recaptured and new sewers will be intrigued and inspired.

Softcover • 8-1/2 x 11
160 pages
200 color photos
150 color illustrations
Item# AWPF • $19.95

More Polarfleece® Adventures
by Nancy Cornwell
Add designer touches to fleece with cutwork, sculpturing, appliqué, pintucking, fancy edge finishes, designer buttonholes, and machine embroidery. Start off with a quick refresher course and end with a chapter filled with fun fleece projects. In between, you'll find a new world of sewing loaded with templates and patterns for the designs featured.

Softcover • 8-1/4 x 10-7/8
160 pages
200 color photos
Item# AWPF2 • $19.95

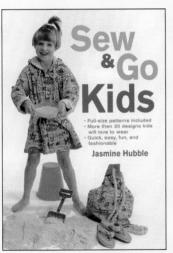

Sew & Go Kids
by Jasmine Hubble
If you love to sew comfortable, fashionable clothing for your kids, but don't have a lot of time, this is the perfect book for you! The author of Sew & Go and Sew & Go Baby gives you more than 30 fun, practical projects like vests, pants, skirts and pajamas (sizes 2 to 8), and, as a bonus, great ideas for playtime. Includes simple step-by-step instructions, helpful illustrations and full-size patterns.

Softcover • 8-1/4 x 10-7/8
96 pages
100 color photos
Item# SWKI • $21.95

Sew & Go Baby
A Collection of Practical Baby Gear Projects
by Jasmine Hubble
Presents 30 practical projects for you to assemble a memorable gift or party for the special baby or toddler in your life. Clear directions, easy-to-follow patterns and full-color photography will enable you to create an entire baby-shower, essential baby gear, clothes, accessories and thoughtful sibling gifts.

Softcover • 8-1/4 x 10-7/8
96 pages
300 Illustrations
Item# SFTB • $19.95

To place a credit card order or for a FREE all-product catalog call
800-258-0929 Dept. CRBR
M-F, 7 am - 8 pm • Sat, 8 am - 2 pm, CST

Shipping and Handling: $3.25 1st book; $2 ea. add'l. Foreign orders $15 per shipment plus $5.95 per book.
Sales tax: CA, IA, IL, PA, TN, VA, WA, WI residents please add appropriate sales tax.
Satisfaction Guarantee: If for any reason you are not completely satisfied with your purchase, simply return it within 14 days and receive a full refund, less shipping.

krause publications
The World's Largest Hobby & Collectibles Publisher

Krause Publications, Offer CRBR
P.O. Box 5009, Iola, WI 54945-5009
www.krausebooks.com
Retailers call toll-free 888-457-2873 ext 880,
M-F, 8 am - 5 pm

CRAFT A
BEAUTIFUL WEDDING
While Adding Your Own Personal Touch

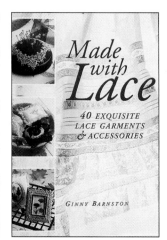

Made With Lace
40 Exquisite Lace Garments and Accessories
by Ginny Barnston

Discover the luxury of lace and the ease of creating your own patterns from this versatile fabric with 40 intriguing and exquisite creations. Each example includes materials and time requirements plus clearly illustrated step-by-step instructions, easy-to-use templates and patterns.
Softcover • 8-1/2 x 11 • 128 pages
Color throughout
MWLQ • $19.95

Bodymapping: The Step-by-Step Guide to Fitting Real Bodies
by Kathy Illian

Learn to make perfectly-fitting garments through Bodymapping, a streamlined fitting process where you drape a poncho-like length of gingham on the body, pin out excess fabric where needed, and mark the body's landmarks on it. Bodymap base pattern can be converted into 15 different fashion blocks.
Softcover • 8-1/4 x 10-7/8 • 120 pages
170 illustrations • 100 color photos
FRB • $19.95

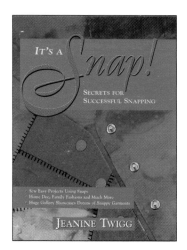

It's A Snap!
Secrets for Successful Snapping
by Jeanine Twigg

A simple and creative alternative to buttons and zippers, this book provides step-by-step methods for attaching snaps - on everything from infant wear to home decor. From basic snapping techniques to garment embellishment, children's games and even creative projects for those with special needs.
Softcover • 8-1/4 x 10-7/8 • 160 pages
100 color photos & 200 illustrations
SNAP • $19.95

Bridal Couture
Fine Sewing Techniques for Wedding Gowns and Evening Wear
by Susan Khalje

Create a fantasy! Susan Khalje guides readers through the principles and techniques of designing, constructing, and embellishing wedding gowns and evening wear. Ideal for the bride-to-be or seamstress, learn how to choose the right fabric, work with lace, or problem solve tricky construction issues.
Softcover • 8-1/4 x 10-7/8 • 160 pages
Color throughout
BCWG • $29.95

Wedding Crafts
40 Charming Ideas for a Unique Personalized Wedding
by Lucinda Ganderton

This ultimate wedding craft book shows how a variety of simple and inexpensive projects can transform a wedding into a uniquely beautiful occasion. Step-by-step photos and instructions make projects easy for wedding, reception and honeymoon. Includes ribboncraft, beadwork, embroidery and decoupage from guest books to hair accessories.
Softcover • 8-1/2 x 11 • 128 pages
300 color photos • 30 color templates
BRCR • $19.95

To place a credit card order or for a FREE all-product catalog call
800-258-0929 Dept. CRBR
M-F, 7 am - 8 pm • Sat, 8 am - 2 pm, CST

Shipping and Handling: $3.25 1st book; $2 ea. add'l. Foreign orders $15 per shipment plus $5.95 per book.
Sales tax: CA, IA, IL, PA, TN, VA, WA, WI residents please add appropriate sales tax.
Satisfaction Guarantee: If for any reason you are not completely satisfied with your purchase, simply return it within 14 days and receive a full refund, less shipping.

krause publications
The World's Largest Hobby & Collectibles Publisher

Krause Publications, Offer CRBR
P.O. Box 5009, Iola, WI 54945-5009
www.krausebooks.com
Retailers call toll-free
888-457-2873 ext 880, M-F, 8 am - 5 pm